Seattle
Mar. 6, 1995
Uwajimaya

1/12   m92057

Cooking

The Book of
RAMEN

Lowcost Gourmet Meals Using
Instant Ramen Noodles

Ron Konzak

The Book of Ramen

Copyright 1993 by Ron Konzak
Illustrations by Ron Konzak
Omnivorous Consultant and Computer Layout: Mickey Molnaire

Published by Turtleback Books
Post Office Box 2012
Friday Harbor, Washington 98250
Tel: (206) 378-3105
Fax: (206) 378-5608

ISBN: 1-883385-13-X

10 9 8 7 6 5 4 3 2 1

Printed in Singapore By
Singapore National Printers

Dedication

This book is dedicated to Mickey Molnaire, my wonderful wife and closest friend, who supports and encourages all my bizarre activities, and to the Japanese Buddhist monks of Nipponzan Myohoji, whose inspiration helps me to view life from a completely different perspective.

TABLE OF CONTENTS

PREFACE vii

ABOUT INSTANT RAMEN
How to Use This Book 5
Noodles 6
Flavor Packets 7
Alternatives to Flavor Packets 10
Basic Broth #1 12
Basic Broth #2 12
Miso Broth 13
Korean Bean Broth 13
Japanese Fish Stock 13
Leftover Flavor Packets 15
Meat 16

SOUPS
Kitsune Ramen 19
Egg Drop Soup 20
Nettle Noodles 22
Ashte Reshte 23
Charlie's Cold Cure 24
Ramen Borshch 25
Almost Instantaneous Corn Chowder 26
Carrot Thread Soup 27
Herbed Cream of Carrot Soup 28
Noodle Gazpacho 29
Spinach Noodle Cream Soup 30
Cauliflower-Cheese Soup 31
Harvest Vegetable Soup 32

SALADS

Chinese Cold Noodle Salad 35
Tuna-Ramen Salad 36
Spinach-Ramen Salad 38
Ginger Ramen Salad 39
Shredded Cabbage Salad 40
Pickled Nettle Greens 40
Garbanzo Salad 41
Cold Asparagus Salad 43
Spinach Salad 43
Shredded Carrot Salad 44
Cucumber-Yogurt Salad 44

MAIN DISHES

Saute Stew 47
Three Minute Stew 48
Ten Minute Stew 49
Hot-Cold Szechuan Noodles 50
Tomato Stew 51
Yaki Ramen 52
Chop Chae 54
Sweet-Sour Tofu 56
Rambalaya 57
Bamboo Shoot Fantasy 58
Chinese Fried Noodles 60
Chow Mein 62
Indonesian Fried Noodles 64
Peanut Sauce 65
Ram Foo Yung 66
Arabic Noodles With Rice 68
Noodles With Greek Celery Sauce 69
Spanakoramen 70
Savory Ramen Custard 72
Ramen Moussaka 74
Curried Noodles 77
Hungarian Noolash 78

Austrian Style Noodles 80
Ramen With Fresh Basil Sauce 81
Italian Spaghetti 82
Zucchini-Nut Noodle Sauce 85
Ramen Ronaldo 86
Guacaramen 87
Ramen Rarebit 89
Noodle Ramenoff 90
Spanish Noodles 92
Ramburger 94
Ramen Meat Loaf 95
Chili Con Ramen 96
Carrot Gravy On Noodles 98
Ramen Vegetable Loaf 99
Ramelet 100
Mee Krob 102
Armenian Wheat-Noodle Pilaf 104
Ramen Quiche 106
Noodle Pie 108
Ramen Dolmeh 110
Maca-Ramen And Cheese 112

DESSERTS

Noodle Pudding 115
Polish Apple-Noodle Pudding 116
Lemon Sauce 117
Maple Ramen 118
Orange-Pineapple Cream Ramen 119
Noodles With Prunes 120
Ramen On A Stick 121
Nutty Noodles 122

APPENDIX

Sources 125
Noodleography 126
Index 127

PREFACE

I think my love affair with instant Ramen began in about 1970 when these packaged noodles first made their appearance in stores on the West Coast. When I introduced visiting relatives to them, they were so intrigued that they actually bought a case of them to take back east, only to find that the Ramen phenomenon would follow them back across the country. Ramen noodles now fill supermarket shelves everywhere. There is hardly a place that they can't be found. Ever so often a new brand appears at a low introductory price, and more people, who know a good deal when they see one, get hooked.

After my initial enthusiasm for this wonder food, I soon began to experiment with variations. Because of my love of cooking, I let my imagination go wild and came up with some pretty unique creations, but it was a long time before I really thought of writing a cookbook. One day a friend suggested, "Why don't you do a cookbook?" I casually replied, "Heck, I *could* write a book about Ramen noodles, I probably have a hundred different ways to fix them." It wasn't until a few hours later that the light went on in my brain and I thought "Why not?"

My background seemed to contain just the right combination of experiences I needed to create this book. Born in an ethnic neighborhood in Detroit, a wide variety of European food was daily fare. I turned vegetarian in my youth and remain so. I served in Japan and Korea in the Air Force where my appetite for Oriental food began, then finally returned to Japan after studying the language and traveled around the country with a Buddhist monk. I stayed in Buddhist temples, dining with the monks in timeless Japanese tradition. I also stayed in private homes, eating casual everyday home cooking. I ate in fine restaurants in Kyoto, small five-seat restaurants in Hiroshima and noodle stands in villages. While in Japan I also ate in Russian, Chinese, East Indian, Mexican, American and Italian restaurants, but I drew the line at Kentucky Fried Chicken and "*Maku Donarudo*" (McDonald's).

Writing this book took me back to all these experiences and led me into a new adventure as I discovered the world of Ramen noodles and collected recipes from my own kitchen and the kitchens of my friends. I wanted this book to be light-hearted and fun as well as useful and hope it keeps you chuckling as you use it. May you enjoy reading this as much as I enjoyed preparing it.

Ron Konzak
Bainbridge Island, Washington

About Instant Ramen

ABOUT INSTANT RAMEN

It's in your market, in your cupboard, on your mind and probably in your tummy. It's probably the biggest instant food fad of our time. It's been called the "Food of the Future", "Manna of the Millions", instant nourishment for busy people on the go, and it costs only a few cents per meal.

Already a familiar sight on our supermarket shelves, these ubiquitous little packages containing an intricately knitted block of dried noodles and a foil packet of powdered flavoring have won the hearts of millions, and why not? Besides their economic advantage, their shelf-life seems to be forever, their flavor is pleasant and hearty, and they are made in convenient individual portions. You don't have to measure a thing, just throw the contents of a package in a pot of water, boil for three minutes or so and you have a meal.

In Japan, where the process for making instant Ramen was invented, it is sometimes referred to as *Gakusei Ryori* or "student cuisine" because of its widespread use by university students

3

kitchen equipment is usually quite limited.

Because of their enthusiastic acceptance in the market place, it wasn't long before instant Ramen skipped over national boundaries and became an international phenomena. Factories that make Ramen noodles can now be found not only in Japan and the U.S., but in Europe, Korea, China, Singapore, Thailand, Malaysia and Indonesia.

Each country's Ramen noodles reflect their own particular flavor preferences. Korean Ramen is highly spiced and often contains packets of black bean sauce. China makes Ramen in Szechuan flavors. Thailand makes very thin, delicate noodles with very hotly spiced packets. Japan prefers the flavor of seafood and mild spices. In the U.S. they are usually available with meat flavors, mushroom flavors or mild spices often referred to as "Oriental flavor".

Ramen noodles originated in China, where all noodles seem to have come from, and are called *Lo-Mein* in Chinese, which means boiled noodles.

Ramen is the Japanese pronunciation of the Chinese Characters for *Lo-Mein*. This Chinese style noodle became such a great favorite in Sapporo, the capital of Japan's northernmost island of Hokkaido, that it is now considered to be their regional dish. Ramen is to Sapporo what baked beans are to Boston. In other countries, the word for Ramen may be different, too. For example, they are called *"Maggi Mee"* in Singapore.

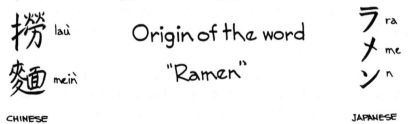

撈 laù
麵 meiñ

CHINESE

Origin of the word
"Ramen"

ラ ra
メ me
ン n

JAPANESE

The process for turning the traditional Ramen noodles into the now familiar instant, packaged noodles was pioneered by Momofuku Ando, the founder of Nissin Foods in Japan. In 1970, Nissin Foods introduced "Top Ramen" to the United States and, as the saying goes, the rest is history. Many other companies introduced Top Ramen clones and even such industry giants such as Lipton and Campbell's began to experiment with Ramen-like products. Fierce competition notwithstanding, Nissin still controls slightly less than half of the U.S. Ramen market and fifteen percent of the world Ramen market of about ten billion dollars annually. At this writing, the average wholesale price for a package of Ramen in the U.S. is only twelve and a half cents.

HOW TO USE THIS BOOK

This book takes a unique approach to Ramen noodles, presenting a number of interesting variations drawn from the rich heritage of noodle dishes found all around the world. Accompanying most recipes are suggestions for appropriate side dishes and beverages and serving hints for ethnic-style meals.

Most of the recipes in this book will provide a main dish for two people. One of the following clock symbols is included with each recipe to indicate the approximate preparation and cooking time:

– Really fast   – About a half hour

– About 15 minutes   – 45 minutes or more

NOODLES

Packaged instant Ramen noodles are usually made of wheat flour, oil and salt. Most popular brands use enriched wheat flour but several brands also offer unbleached flour, whole wheat, buckwheat and rice flour. Most of the manufacturers of instant Ramen deep-fry their noodles in oil, which accounts for the oil listed in the ingredients. Many different kinds of oil are used, usually corn, soy or cottonseed oil, but also sometimes palm or coconut oil, which are highly saturated. Persons on a low cholesterol diet should be aware of this. It is always a good idea to read the ingredients before assuming that all instant Ramen packages are the same.

For people who are of the "organic foods" persuasion, there are brands sold through health food stores and community co-ops that use natural ingredients. In the back of this book you will find a list of some of these different brands.

Some Ramen-type noodles are available that are air-dried rather than deep-fried. Unfortunately, it is difficult to tell which ones are which, but if the noodle ingredients list oil, I assume that the noodles are deep-fried. Some brands will state on the package that they are air-dried.

It is a common belief that each package of Ramen contains one incredibly long noodle curled and coiled into a solid block. I have found that this is not the case. After selecting a package of Ramen at random and carefully boiling and taking it apart, I found that the package contained eighty strands of curly noodles 5/64″ (2 mm.) diameter that, when straightened out, measured approximately 16″ (40 cm.) in length. This would indicate that the noodle dough (sometimes called alimentary paste) was extruded through eighty nipples into continuous rows, and cut into uniform lengths. The eighty, curly noodles, cut to length, were then folded over once before being dropped into a mold, lightly fried, dried, and packaged with a flavor packet insert.

Each package, when boiled, stretched out and laid end to end, contains about 100 linear feet of noodles. A million and a quarter packages of Ramen, boiled and placed end to end can encircle the earth at the equator. All the Ramen sold in the world in one single day could make 490 round trips around the world.

While we are on the subject of long noodles, you can see how a sixteen inch long noodle can be a problem in some recipes. In traditional Japanese meals, long noodles are graceful and easily eaten with chopsticks while sipping the broth directly from the bowl, but in the case where other ingredients are mixed with the noodles it is better to use short noodles. In some cases you may even want it to be granular. This is easily done by crushing the uncooked noodles while they are still in their unopened bag.

Most instructions on Ramen packages say to cook noodles in boiling water for three minutes. If you like your noodles slightly on the firm side this is fine. Cook them longer if you prefer softer noodles. Also, the noodles get a little fatter the longer you cook them.

FLAVOR PACKETS

Ramen noodles always come with a flavor packet, usually made of sealed foil or plastic containing spices and dried foods to flavor the broth in which the noodles are cooked. Usually, all the noodles of any particular brand are identical and get their characteristic flavor from the contents of this little package. Most flavorings are identical except for the main flavoring agent which may be a beef or chicken extract, mushroom extract, "oriental spices", etc. Almost all the flavor packets for Ramen brands made in the U. S. come from the same company.

The main flavor carrier is Hydrolyzed Vegetable Protein (HVP), a soybean extract. Then there is the flavor enhancing trio, Monosodium Glutamate (MSG), Disodium Inosynate and Disodium Guanylate. MSG makes up the greatest volume of these and, in combination with the other two, creates the taste that most people seem to enjoy.

Here is some information that I have found about the ingredients you will most likely see listed on your Ramen package.

Hydrolyzed vegetable protein (HVP): Also known as *hydrolyzed plant protein*. An extract of soybean made in a process similar to soy sauce, but where soy sauce is naturally fermented, HVP is chemically digested. It is generally regarded as safe for adults, but sometimes causes an allergic reaction in infants.

Monosodium glutamate (MSG): Always controversial but never really proven harmful or non-harmful. Some people have an allergy to it and experience temporary reactions called the "Chinese restaurant syndrome" (CRS), Others are not bothered by it. It is particularly reactive when taken in a broth on an empty stomach. People who are sensitive to wheat, corn or sugar beets should avoid it. MSG is made from soybeans. Since it is a sodium, it is wise to watch your intake as you would when you use salt.

Disodium inosynate, disodium guanylate, despite their formidable sounding names, are generally accepted safe flavor enhancers. They are usually used in combination with MSG and usually comprise .003% to .05% of the volume of the flavor packets. The reason these additives are so minute in quantity is because their taste is very intense and the cost is very high.

No, they are not a derivative of guano, but are made by a fermentation process or chemical synthesis of dried fish. If you are a vegetarian and would object to a microscopic amount of fish in your food, you may want to take this into consideration.

Caramel is made by heating sugar and is used as a coloring agent to create a rich brown color. It is as safe as any other sugar.

Glucose is just another type of sugar.

Thiamin is vitamin B, a natural ingredient found in wheat germ, peas, pork and yeast. Added to increase the nutritive value of wheat, it's usually in the form of thiamin mononitrate and thiamin hydrochloride.

Guar gum comes from the Guar plant (similar to the soybean plant) and is used as a thickener. It is safe and digestible.

Hydrogenation is a reaction of oils to hydrogen which converts them from a liquid to a semi-liquid. All fats should be used in moderation, particularly saturated fats. Palm and coconut oils are higher in saturation than butter or beef fat and should be used in moderation to avoid high cholesterol levels.

There, now that it's out in the open, you can decide for yourself whether or not you want to use the flavor packet provided with the Ramen. Of course, you can use just a portion of the packet, (sometimes I find the taste to be a bit intense), or not at all and make your own quick stock. Remember, the reason for using Ramen is to keep it simple, keep it quick and keep it fun. This rules out cooking a soup bone or boiling down a vegetable stock for hours and hours. Here are some ideas for some quick, easy alternatives to flavor packets:

ALTERNATIVES TO FLAVOR PACKETS

Of course, the simplest substitute is to find bouillon that you like and stock up on it. Stir them in just as you would the enclosed flavor packets. Some bouillons come in bulk or loose in jars. Any of these can be used where the recipe calls for a "flavor packet". If you have a particular dietary preference, you can surely find the bouillon that's really "you" at a health food store or community co-op. Many markets are now carrying foods in bulk containers and often soup-mix powders can be found there. Although they are not flavor packets, they are designed to be fast and simple. Use wherever a flavor packet is called for on the Ramen package or in the recipes of this book.

Tokyo eats Ramen

Ramen eats Tokyo

Basic Broth #1

1 tsp.	*Bouillon**
1 Tbsp.	*Soy sauce*
1/4 tsp.	*Garlic powder*
1/2 tsp.	*Onion powder*
1 Tbsp.	*Soy sauce*
	Salt and pepper to taste

* Maggi seasoning, Dr. Bronners Balanced mineral bouillon or your favorite bouillon.

Simply put ingredients into recipe where flavor packet is called for.

Basic Broth #2

1 large	*Shiitake mushroom*
1 Tbsp.	*Soy sauce*
1 piece	*Kombu, (dried Kelp)*
1/4 tsp.	*Garlic powder*
1/2 tsp.	*Onion powder*
1/4 tsp.	*Powdered ginger*
	Salt and pepper to taste

Buzz up one dried *Shiitake* mushroom in a blender until powdered. Put all ingredients into recipe where a flavor packet is called for. Remove piece of *Kombu* as soon as water starts to boil so it doesn't taste too strong.

Miso Broth

Miso is a flavoring paste made of fermented soybeans. To make *miso* broth, add one tablespoon of *miso* paste to any of these broths or to a flavor packet and mix in after the stock has been boiled. There are many different kinds of *miso* paste. Some people consider the dark ones too strong and prefer some of the lighter varieties, especially some of the new so-called "gourmet" *miso* pastes with herbs, spices or other interesting flavors. Boiling *miso* destroys its nutritive value.

Korean Black Bean Broth

Korean black bean paste is available at many oriental food stores that sell Japanese foods. Simply add a teaspoon of this thick, molasses-like paste to any of these broths to make a hearty bean broth.

Japanese Fish Stock

1/4 cup	*Dashi (Dry Bonito flakes)*
1/2 piece	*Kombu, (dried Kelp)*

Put one-half piece of *Kombu*, about 2 inches by 4 inches, In two cups of water and bring to a boil. Take *Kombu* out as soon as the water boils to keep it from getting too strong, add *Dashi* and take off heat. When *Dashi* settles to the bottom, strain out and pour over cooked drained Ramen noodles.

Marco Polo brings noodles to the west from China

Here are some additional ingredients that you can add to the basic stocks that may appeal to your taste buds.

1/4 tsp.	*Ginger, powdered or*
1 tsp.	*Ginger, fresh grated*
1 dash	*Lemon juice*
1/2 tsp.	*Sesame oil, toasted*
1 dash	*Worcestershire sauce*
1 dash	*Tabasco sauce*
1/2 tsp.	*Curry powder*

It's a good idea to experiment with these ingredients and find the stock most to your liking and keep it in a handy spot next to your Ramen-making operation.

LEFTOVER FLAVOR PACKETS

Some of the recipes in this book do not call for the use of a flavor packet and you might end up with a little collection of extra flavor packets before you know it. They come in handy, however if you ever want to make a quick gravy or need some soup stock.

To make a gravy, simply add a flavor packet and a tablespoon of cornstarch to a cup and a half of cold water and bring to a boil, stirring frequently just before it boils.

For a soup stock, add a flavor packet to two cups of water and stir well. Use in your favorite soup recipe where soup stock or consomme is called for.

MEAT

All of these recipes were designed to be "vegetarian-friendly" and need no meat to complete their flavor. However, this is not intended to be a vegetarian cook-book. There is no question that those who eat meat would enjoy the addition of their favorite meat, or those meats appropriate to the particular recipe in use. For this reason, many of these recipes may contain meat. Unless otherwise noted, simply omit the meat to make the meal vegetarian.

Meatless protein sources may also be used. *Tofu* in its most simple block-style – firm, soft, silken – is probably the most widely known and available, but is also worth pursuing in lesser known forms, like deep-fried tofu pouches (called *Aburage* in Japanese), which tend to resemble and behave more like meat or eggs in the cooking process.

Meatless vegetable burgers and other meat look-alike products are now produced by several manufactureres. Textured vegetable protein (TVP), found in natural food stores, makes a good substitute for ground beef. *Seitan,* or "wheat-meat", made from wheat gluten, is found in oriental groceries and can take the place of chicken. *Tempeh,* a fermented soybean loaf, can be fried in slices, like bacon, or stewed in cubes.

Soups

⏱ **Kitsune Ramen**

This is originally a way of preparing the thick Japanese Udon noodles, but adapts very well to instant Ramen. *Kitsune* means "Fox" in Japanese and refers to the reddish-brown color of the fried bean curd.

1 Pkg.	*Ramen noodles*
	Japanese fish stock (page 13)
1 tsp.	*Soy sauce*
1 tsp.	*Mirin or white wine.*
I slice	*Aburage (fried bean curd)*
3 med.	*Spinach leaves, fresh*
	Hot pepper to taste

In a small saucepan, boil noodles and Japanese fish stock in 2 cups of water for 5 minutes.

Cut *aburage* into thin strips. (*Aburage,* usually available in Japanese import shops, is a little sack made of fried bean curd about 1-1/2 inches square that is used for making *sushi*.) Cut the spinach leaves into strips also. Put these into the soup while still hot. Add other seasonings. You can also make this with a stock of the enclosed flavor packet instead of the Japanese fish stock.

⏱ **Egg Drop Soup**

Have you started accumulating any left-over flavor packets yet? Here's a good way to put them to use. It goes well with any Chinese or Japanese meal.

1	*Flavor packet*
2 cups	*Water*
1	*Egg*
1 tsp	*White wine or Sake*
1	*Green onion, chopped*

Bring flavor packet, water and wine to boil. Mix egg in a bowl with a fork, but do not beat. Pour egg slowly into gently boiling soup, a little at a time. Take off heat when all the egg turns into threads.

Garnish with chopped green onion.

⏱ **Nettle Noodles**

Stinging nettles are usually regarded as a nuisance, but if they happen to grow on your property you can get rid of them by eating them. They have a pleasant flavor.

1 Pkg.	*Ramen noodles*
20 Tops	*Stinging nettles, fresh*
1 tsp.	*Soy sauce*
1 tsp.	*Onion powder*
1 tsp.	*Garlic powder*
	Salt and pepper to taste

Nettles grow from early spring until mid summer. The earlier plants are the choicest. Pick the new, top cluster of leaves (About 6 leaves) from 20 plants. Use gloves and put tops in a bag until ready to use. One slip and you will itch all day. Wash leaves in a strainer and boil in a small saucepan in 2 cups of water. They will lose their stinging properties in the hot water. Boil for 3 minutes then remove the greens. Use the greens in the recipe for "Pickled Nettle Greens" on page 40.

Use the broth to cook the Ramen noodles. Season with remaining ingredients

⊕ Ashte Reshte

Persian food is characterized by its use of sweet, rather than hot, spices and by the absence of garlic. To make this soup quickly, use canned lentils and black-eyed peas or cook them ahead, boiling 1/4 cup of each for 30 minutes. Believe me, it's worth the effort!

1 Pkg.	*Ramen noodles*
1/2 cup	*Cooked lentils*
1/2 cup	*Cooked black-eyed peas*
1/4 cup	*Chopped onion*
2 tsp.	*Oil*
1 Tbsp.	*Dried parsley*
2 Dashes	*Cinnamon*
1 Pinch	*Dried mint*
1	*Flavor packet*
	Salt and black pepper to taste

In a medium saucepan, fry the onions in the oil with a dash of cinnamon and pepper.

When the onions are transparent, add 1-1/2 cups of water and a package of Ramen noodles. (Crush them while still in the package so they will not be too long.) Also add the lentils, peas, flavor packet, mint, parsley and another dash of cinnamon. Bring to boil and cook for 10 minutes. Add a little water, if needed, to make a hearty, stew-like soup.

Although this soup can be a complete meal as it is, serving it with Cucumber-Yogurt Salad (Page 44) will turn your meal into a memorable feast.

23

◷ **Charlie's Cold Cure**

I make no medical claims for this, but it did make me feel a lot better when I had a bad cold. My friend Charlie claims that two of these a day for a couple days in a row and your cold is history.

1 Pkg.	*Ramen noodles*
1	*Flavor packet*
3 Tbsp.	*Garlic, minced*
1 Tbsp.	*Butter or Margarine*
5 Slices	*Ginger root, minced*
1/4 tsp.	*Cayenne pepper*

Boil all ingredients together in two cups of water. You can substitute 2 ounces of garlic spread concentrate for the minced garlic and butter or margarine. Try at least two servings per day until cold is better. I guarantee a really intense experience.

Ⓘ Ramen Borshch

This soup is based on a Polish *borshch* recipe that has been in my family for generations.

While you can have this dish ready to eat in a half an hour, it tastes better if it cooks slowly. It tastes best if you can wait till the next day, storing it overnight in the fridge and reheating. Don't cover the pan while it is cooking, or boil too vigorously – the beets will lose their beautiful color and turn a murky brown.

1 Pkg.	*Ramen, broken up*
1	*Flavor packet*
2 1/2 cups	*Water*
1 can	*Diced beets (16 oz.)*
2 Tbsp.	*Butter or Margarine*
2 tsp.	*Onion powder*
3 Tbsp.	*Cider vinegar or white vinegar*
1 tsp.	*Sugar*
2	*Fresh mushrooms, sliced thin*
2/3 cup	*Milk*
1 tsp.	*Flour*
	Salt
	Sour cream for garnish

Bring water to boil in a saucepan. Add the ramen, flavor packet, beets, butter, onion powder, cider vinegar, sugar and mushrooms. Cook over low heat, uncovered, for an hour.

Just before serving, mix the flour and milk together and stir into the soup for thickening. Salt to taste. Serve with a dollop of sour cream.

⏱ Almost Instantaneous Corn Chowder

A really hearty soup that can be prepared in less than 10 minutes.

1 Pkg.	Ramen noodles, broken up
1	Flavor packet
2 cups	Water
16 oz can	Cream-style corn
1/4 tsp.	Powdered ginger
1/4 tsp.	Curry powder
1/4 tsp.	Onion powder
1/4 tsp.	Garlic powder
1/2 cup	Milk or soymilk
1/2 cup	Cheddar cheese, grated
	Salt and pepper to taste
	Parsley for garnish (optional)

In a medium saucepan, bring 2 cups of water to a boil. Add ramen and flavor packet and cook for 5 minutes. Mix in cream-style corn, ginger, curry powder, onion and garlic powder and milk. Heat over medium heat. If using real milk, don't let the soup boil.

When all the ingredients are heated through, add the grated cheese and mix until it melts. Salt and pepper to taste. Adjust with more milk if soup is too thick. Garnish with a sprig of parsley.

⏱ **Carrot Thread Soup**

Even though there are three recipes in this book with carrots as the main ingredients, they are all quite different. The secret to this variety is the texture of the carrots. The carrots in this recipe are cut into noodle-like "threads" by laying the carrot flat against a standard box grater (coarse side) and drawing the carrot back and forth along its length.

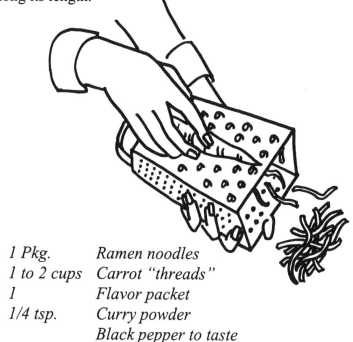

1 Pkg.	*Ramen noodles*
1 to 2 cups	*Carrot "threads"*
1	*Flavor packet*
1/4 tsp.	*Curry powder*
	Black pepper to taste

In a small saucepan, boil noodles, carrot threads and flavor packet in water for 5 minutes.

Season with curry powder, for just a touch of spiciness, and black pepper.

Herbed Cream of Carrot Soup

1 Pkg.	Ramen noodles
1	Flavor packet
1/2 cups	Water
3	Large carrots, sliced thin
1/2 tsp.	Garlic powder
1/2 tsp.	Onion powder
1 Tbsp.	Dill weed
1/4 tsp.	Marjoram
1/2 tsp.	Thyme
1 tsp.	Sweet paprika
1/3 cup	Milk or soymilk
1 Tbsp.	Sherry or white wine
1 Tbsp.	Butter or margarine
	Salt or pepper to taste

In a medium saucepan, bring water to boil and add all ingredients except milk, sherry and butter. Cook over medium high heat, covered, until carrots are very soft.

In a blender or food processor, puree the mixture. Return to saucepan and add milk, sherry, butter, salt and pepper. Taste and adjust any other flavorings.

◐ Noodle Gazpacho

Here's another soup for the gardener with an exploding garden. All the vegetables, as well as the noodles, are uncooked in this Ramen version of a traditional Spanish cold summer soup.

1 Pkg.	*Ramen noodles*
1	*Large tomato, diced*
1/2 cup	*Cucumber, diced*
1/2 cup	*Green pepper, diced*
1/4 cup	*Onion, chopped*
1 Clove	*Garlic, crushed*
1 Tbsp.	*Wine vinegar*
1 Tbsp.	*Olive oil*
1 Tbsp.	*Lime juice*
1	*Flavor packet*
	Salt and pepper to taste.

Crush Ramen in the package until it is very small. Add all the ingredients in a large bowl with 2 1/2 cups of water. Chill for half an hour.

You can make the texture more interesting if you, just before serving, take out 1 cup of the mixture and blend it in a blender, and stir it back into the soup.

Serve with an ice cube floating in each bowl.

⏀ **Spinach Noodle Cream Soup**

Everyone knows that spinach is good for you. It also lends a nice flavor to this soup, as well as turning it a vivid green. If you object to the intense green color, wear green-tinted glasses.

1 Pkg.	*Ramen*
1/2 Pkg.	*Spinach, frozen*
1	*Flavor packet*
1/2 tsp.	*Onion powder*
1/2 tsp.	*Garlic powder*
1/4 tsp.	*Paprika*
Dash	*Nutmeg*
1/4 tsp.	*Marjoram*
1/4 tsp.	*Thyme*
1/4 tsp.	*Rosemary*
1 cup	*Cream or Milk*
1 Tbsp.	*Parmesan cheese, grated*
	Salt and pepper to taste

In a small saucepan, boil 2 cups of water with noodles, spinach and flavor packet for 7 to 10 minutes.

Add all ingredients except grated cheese and puree in blender.

Return to heat briefly until heated through. Add a little more milk or water if soup is too thick.

Garnish each serving with a sprinkling of grated Parmesan cheese and a dash of paprika.

⏱ **Cauliflower-Cheese Soup**

Hearty is the word for this soup. The perfect winter soup for watching snow fall on your garden from your kitchen window. Despite the big flavor, this is a very simple recipe and can be made in little more than 5 minutes.

1 Pkg.	*Ramen noodles*
1 cup	*Cauliflower, chopped fine*
1/4 cup	*Cheddar cheese, grated*
1/4 cup	*Milk*
1	*Flavor packet*

In a saucepan, boil Ramen, cauliflower and flavor packet together in 2 cups of water for 5 minutes. Remove from heat.

Stir in cheese. (Do not boil once the cheese and milk have been added.)

Thin with milk.

Ra-men   noodles

◑ Harvest Vegetable Soup

If you are a gardener like I am, there are times when your garden seems to go out of control and you have more vegetables than you know what to do with. This is not so much a fixed recipe as an inspiration for what to do with a bounty of vegetables and a package of Ramen.

1 Pkg.	*Ramen noodles*
1	*Flavor packet*
Any combination of the following:	
1	*Tomato, fresh, large*
1	*Zucchini, medium*
1	*Carrot, medium, sliced*
1	*Potato, small, cubed*
1/2 cup	*Green onion*
1/2 cup	*Green beans, cut in bite-sized pieces*

You can't go wrong. Any or all of these will make a fine soup. Don't be too literal with the ingredients, as not all of these vegetables will be in season simultaneously.

Start with 2 cups of water, Ramen noodles broken up fine and a flavor packet. Start loading up the pot with vegetables.

Plunge fresh tomato in boiling water for a minute to loosen the skin. Peel and chop.

Add other vegetables and boil until tender. Short cooking time veggies like zucchini can be added later to avoid overcooking.

If you have to add more water because of the multitude of vegetables, add another flavor packet or bouillon cube.

Salads

⊕ Chinese Cold Noodle Salad

1 Pkg.	*Ramen noodles*
1/4 cup	*Cucumber slices*
1-1/2 tsp.	*Sugar*
1 Tbsp.	*Soy sauce*
2 tsp.	*Rice vinegar*
1 tsp.	*Sesame oil, toasted*
1	*Green onion, minced*
1/4 tsp.	*Ginger, powdered*
1/4 cup	*Ham, cooked*
1 Tbsp.	*Sesame seeds, white*

In a small saucepan, boil noodles in 2 cups of water for five minutes. When noodles are done, put into a strainer, rinse with cold water and let drain for a few minutes, shaking the water out to make them as dry as possible.

Cut cucumber and ham into thin "matchsticks". Put sesame seeds in a small dry saucepan, cover and toast over high heat, shaking constantly until you can hear them popping. Take off heat and put into a mortar, crush lightly with a pestle to release flavor. Sprinkle the cucumbers and ham over the noodles, mix the rest of the ingredients into a dressing and pour over the salad.

Tuna Ramen Salad

This home-style pasta salad is a refreshing snack that goes well on hot summer days and is a winner at potluck dinners. Serve with buttered Italian or French bread.

1 Pkg.	*Ramen noodles*
1 Can	*Tuna (in oil) 6.5 oz.*
1 Can	*Olives, black, sliced, 2.25 oz.*
3 Tbsp.	*Onions, finely chopped*
2 1/3 Tbsp.	*Mayonnaise*
1/8 tsp.	*Mustard, Dijon*
1 Tbsp.	*Vinegar, red wine*
2 Tbsp.	*Garlic powder*
1 tsp.	*Basil*
1/4 tsp.	*Oregano*
1/4 tsp.	*Dillweed*
1 Pinch	*Allspice*
3 Tbsp.	*Romano or Parmesan cheese*
	Salt and pepper to taste

In a small saucepan, boil noodles in 2 cups of water for five minutes. When noodles are done, rinse in strainer with cold water and let drain for a few minutes, shaking the water out to make them as dry as possible.

Drain tuna and put in a large mixing bowl. Flake with a fork. Chop onions and celery finely and put into bowl. Add mayonnaise, mustard,vinegar and spices. Combine thoroughly. Add noodles and toss together until thoroughly mixed. Note: This is one meal that won't turn into a passable vegetarian dish by omitting the tuna.

Ramen and Juliet

⏱ Spinach Ramen Salad

I was a bit skeptical when first offered this salad made with raw, uncooked Ramen noodles, but after tasting it a broad smile crossed my face. A most unusual way to use instant Ramen, but a real treat!

1 Pkg.	*Ramen noodles*
1 bunch	*Spinach, fresh*
1 med.	*Tomato*
1 med.	*Avocado*
1	*Flavor packet*
3 Tbsp.	*Olive oil*
1 Tbsp.	*Vinegar*
1/2 tsp.	*Garlic powder*

Knead unopened package of Ramen noodles until broken up fine.

Mix together olive oil, vinegar, garlic powder and contents of flavor packet. Put into small covered container and shake well.

Remove stems from spinach, wash and tear into small pieces. Add sliced tomatoes, sliced avocados, Ramen and dressing mixture. Toss well.

Ginger Ramen Salad

1 Pkg.	*Ramen noodles, crushed*
1/2	*Flavor packet*
1 inch	*Fresh ginger root, coarsely chopped*
1 1/2 cup	*Water*
2 Cloves	*Garlic*
2 Tbsp.	*Sesame seeds*
2 Tsp.	*Oil (anything but olive)*
2 Tsp.	*Soy sauce*
1 Tbsp.	*Mirin, sake or white wine*
1/2 cup	*Frozen peas*
2	*Green onions, chopped fine*
	A few drops of Sesame oil

Blend water, ginger and garlic at high speed. Transfer to saucepan and bring to boil. Add Ramen and 1/2 flavor packet and cook over medium heat until liquid is absorbed.

In a small bowl combine oil, soy sauce, mirin and sesame oil.

Put noodles in a larger bowl. Add sauce, peas and green onion and sesame seeds and toss together.

SALADS TO ACCOMPANY RAMEN DISHES

You may like a non-Ramen salad to balance out your meal.

◔ Shredded Cabbage Salad

1 cup	*Cabbage, shredded*
1/4 cup	*Rice vinegar*
1 tsp.	*Sugar*

Mix vinegar and sugar together well, pour over cabbage. Use either white or red cabbage.

◔ Pickled Nettle Greens

	Cooked nettle greens*
1 Tbsp.	*Rice vinegar*
1 Tbsp.	*Soy sauce*
1/4 tsp.	*Ginger, fresh grated*
1 Tbsp.	*Sesame seeds, crushed, roasted*

*See "Nettle Noodles" on page 22 and use the nettle greens as prepared and left over from that recipe.

Mix all ingredients together and keep in a closed jar in the refrigerator. An excellent pickle to use with Japanese food. Let marinate for a few hours. Will keep for several weeks.

⊕ Garbanzo Salad

14 oz can	*Garbanzo beans*
1	*Tomato, medium , chopped*
1/2 cup	*Onion, chopped*
1 Clove	*Garlic, minced*
3 Tbsp.	*Olive oil*
1 Tbsp.	*Rosemary, dried and crushed*
	Salt and pepper to taste

Drain beans and put in bowl.

Fry onions and garlic until soft and add to bowl. Add the rest of the ingredients and mix well.

The longer this dish gets to stand at room temperature before eating, at least 1 to 2 hours, the better the flavors blend together.

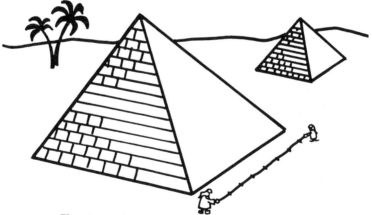

Each side of the pyramid of Cheops is the total length of noodles in 7½ packages of instant Ramen.

Cold Asparagus Salad

1/4 lb.	*Asparagus, Fresh*
1/4 cup	*Soy sauce*
1 Tbsp.	*Rice vinegar*
1/2 tsp.	*Sugar*

Steam whole asparagus spears for ten minutes. Allow to cool in refrigerator. Mix other ingredients together well and pour over asparagus.

Sesame Spinach Salad

2 cups	*Spinach leaves, fresh*
1/2	*Flavor packet*
1/2 cup	*Water*
1 Tbsp.	*Soy sauce*
1 Tbsp.	*Sesame seeds*
1 tsp.	*Sugar*

Remove stems from spinach, cut into bite size pieces and steam until they just start to soften.

Toast sesame seeds in a small, dry, covered saucepan on high heat, shaking constantly to keep from burning. After the seeds have popped, crush lightly in a mortar with a pestle to release flavor. Mix in with other ingredients. Pour over spinach. (Served cold)

⏱ Shredded Carrot Salad

1 med.	*Carrot*
1 Tbsp.	*Vinegar*
1 tsp.	*Sugar*
	Salt to taste

Shred one whole medium sized carrot. Sprinkle with vinegar, sugar and salt. Stir together.

⏱ Cucumber-Yogurt Salad

A cool accompaniment to Indian curries and spicy Middle Eastern dishes.

1	*Cucumber*
1 cup	*Yogurt*
1 Tbsp.	*Mint, dried*
1 Tbsp.	*Dill weed, dried*
	Salt and Pepper to taste.

Peel and grate cucumber into a bowl. Drain off the liquid, pressing the grated cucumber to expel as much as possible. Add the rest of the ingredients and mix together.

Main Dishes

⊕ Saute Stew

1 Pkg.	*Ramen noodles*
1	*Flavor packet*
1/4 cup	*Chopped onions*
1/4 cup	*Sliced mushrooms*
1/4 cup	*Chopped green peppers*
1	*Celery stalk*
1 tsp.	*Cornstarch*
Optional:	
1/4 cup	*Diced cooked meat (your favorite)*
1/4 cup	*Tiny shrimp*

Cook the noodles and flavor packet together with one cup of water.

While they are cooking, saute meat or shrimp in 1 tbsp. oil for a few minutes, then add the onions, mushroom slices, green pepper, and the celery (sliced thin, diagonally) and stir-fry together in a cast iron frying pan or *wok* for two minutes. Add to the cooked noodles and mix together.

Mix the cornstarch with a small amount of cold water and mix until smooth, then add to the stew and bring to a boil and stir until thickened.

⊘ **Three Minute Stew**

1 Pkg.	*Ramen noodles*
1	*Flavor packet*
1/4 cup	*Tofu, diced*
1/4 cup	*Frozen peas or corn*
1	*Green onion, chopped*

Cook the noodles with the flavor packet according to the instructions on the package, using 2 cups of water if you like it soup-like, as a broth, or 1 cup if you like it as a cooked noodle dish.

While this is cooking, put the *tofu* and frozen vegetables in the bottom of a bowl and chop up a scallion.

When the noodles are done, pour them over the cold vegetables and *tofu* in the bowl, mix together well and sprinkle the green onions on top.

The vegetables and *tofu* will cool the stew slightly, enabling you to eat on the run, and the *tofu* and peas (legumes) will combine with the noodles (grains) to form a complete protein. Fast, tasty and nutritious.

⏲ Ten Minute Stew

1 Pkg.	*Ramen noodles*
1	*Flavor packet*
1/4 cup	*Chopped onions*
1/2 cup	*Cauliflower florets*
1	*Carrot, med. size*
1	*Zucchini, small*

Slice the carrots and zucchini at 45 degree angle, 1/4″ and 1/2″ thick respectively.

Cook all the ingredients together in a small saucepan until cooked to your satisfaction, from 7 to 10 minutes. Adjust the amount of water, starting with 1-1/2 cups of water, to make your choice of a soup-like or stew-like dish.

Noodle doodle

Hot-cold Szechuan Noodles

Hot-cold means that the noodles are served ice-cold and the sauce is hotly spiced. This is a great snack to have while viewing the moon on a hot summer night and listening to the sound of crickets.

1 Pkg.	Ramen noodles
1/2 cup	Bean sprouts
1 Tbsp.	Sesame oil, toasted
1 tsp.	Hot pepper oil
1 tsp.	Ginger, powdered
1 tsp.	Garlic powder
1 Tbsp.	Vinegar
	Salt and pepper to taste
1	Green onion, chopped
1/4 cup	Chicken, cooked and chopped
1 Tbsp.	Peanuts, chopped

In a small saucepan, boil noodles in 2 cups of water for five minutes. When noodles are done, put into a strainer, rinse with cold water and let drain for a few minutes, shaking the water out to make them as dry as possible. Cool in a refrigerator until cold.

Blanch bean sprouts in boiling water for 10 seconds. Rinse in cold water and place on top of the cold noodles in a bowl.

Mix seasonings together to make a sauce. Spoon over noodles and sprouts.

Garnish with chicken, chopped peanuts and chopped green onion. Serve with a tall glass of cold beer.

⏱ **Tomato Stew**

A hearty tomato stew hits the spot on a cold winter day. Serve this with a hot bread roll and butter.

1 Pkg.	*Ramen noodles*
1/4 cup	*Onion, chopped*
1/4 cup	*Celery, chopped*
2 cups	*Canned tomatoes*
1 cup	*Water*
1	*Flavor packet*
1 tsp.	*Butter*
1/2 tsp	*Sugar*
1 tsp.	*Cornstarch*
1/2 tsp	*Basil*

Chop up the tomatoes and put tomatoes and liquid into a sauce pan with the onion and celery. Add flavor packet, butter, sugar, and basil.

Break Ramen noodles into quarters in unopened package. Mix with all other ingredients and bring to a boil. Reduce heat and simmer for ten minutes.

Mix cornstarch with a small amount of cold water and mix until smooth. Add to the pot and boil, stirring until thickened.

⏁ **Yaki Ramen**

Yaki Soba is made on a griddle and sold in booths at many outdoor gatherings in Japanese-American communities. *Yaki Ramen* is just as good. As a matter of fact, *Yaki Soba* is a misnomer as *sob*a noodles are not used. The noodles used are very similar to Ramen.

1 Pkg.	*Ramen noodles*
1/2 cup	*Onions, sliced into crescents*
1	*Flavor packet*
1 tsp.	*Worcestershire Sauce*
Optional:	
1 Large	*Shiitake mushroom, dried*
1/4 cup	*Pork, cut into thin strips*
1/2 cup	*Cabbage, thinly sliced*

In a small saucepan, boil noodles in 2 cups of water for five minutes. When noodles are done, put into a strainer, rinse with cold water and let drain for a few minutes, shaking the water out to make them as dry as possible.

A *wok* is the best way to make Yaki Ramen, but it can also be done in a cast iron skillet. In a *wok*, the stir-frying can be done with a very small amount of oil, in a skillet you may have to use more oil.

If using cabbage, slice thinly. Reconstitute *shiitake* mushroom by placing in a dish of warm water till soft. Cut cap into thin, long slices. Discard the stem, which is very tough.

Heat oil in a *wok* or skillet until it almost starts to smoke. Stir-fry onions and any other ingredients together. Pour

52

noodles on top of other ingredients and sprinkle contents of flavor packet over it.

Quickly stir-fry all ingredients together for about 2 minutes.

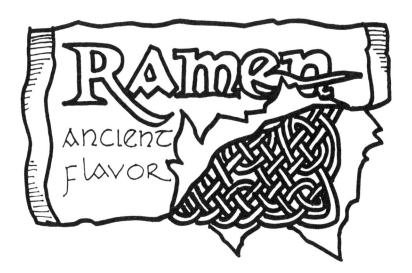

Ancient Ramen package found in a tomb of a Celtic Chieftain

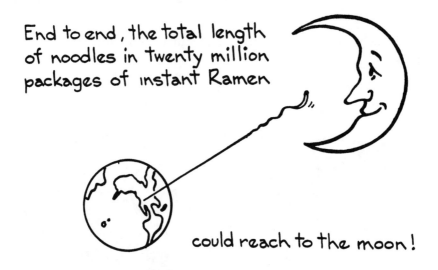

End to end, the total length of noodles in twenty million packages of instant Ramen could reach to the moon!

⊕ Chop Chae

A very popular dish in Korea, this Ramen noodle version closely approximates the original recipe.

1 Pkg.	*Ramen noodles*
1/2 cup	*String beans, French style,*
1 Med.	*Carrot*
1/2 cup	*Onions, sliced into thin crescents*
1 Stalk	*Celery*
1/4 cup	*Mushrooms*
1/4 cup	*Beef, sliced into strips*

1/4 cup	*Bamboo Shoots*
1 Tbsp.	*Soy sauce*
2 Tbsp.	*Sugar*
1	*Green onion*
1 Clove	*Garlic, chopped*
1 Tbsp.	*Sesame oil*
1	*Egg*
1 Tbsp.	*Sesame seeds,roasted*

In a small saucepan, boil noodles in 2 cups of water for 5 minutes. When noodles are done, put into a strainer, rinse with cold water and let drain for a few minutes, shaking the water out to make them as dry as possible.

If frozen beans are used, thaw out and steam with other vegetables. If fresh beans are used, cut them into thin strips resembling noodles. (There is actually an inexpensive kitchen gadget called a French bean cutter that can make this job easier.)

Cut bamboo shoots into "matchsticks" 2″ long.

Steam green beans, carrots and bamboo shoots until tender.

Cut onion into thin crescents. Cut celery, mushrooms and beef also into matchstick-size pieces. Saute beef for one minute in sesame oil. Add onion, celery and mushrooms and stir-fry together on high heat.

After one minute, add noodles and fry together for another minute. Mix cooked vegetables in and take off heat.

Mix soy sauce, sugar, chopped garlic and green onion together and stir into food mixture.

Garnish with fried egg, cut into thin strips, matchstick size, and crushed sesame seeds.

⊕ Sweet-Sour Tofu

1 Pkg.	*Ramen noodles*
1/4 cup	*Pineapple, chopped*
1/2 cup	*Tofu, firm, diced*
1/4 cup	*Green pepper, diced*
1	*Onion, small*
1 Tbsp.	*Sugar*
1 Tbsp.	*Vinegar*
1-1/2 tsp.	*Cornstarch*
1/2 cup	*Pineapple juice*
1 Tbsp.	*Oil*

In a small saucepan, boil noodles in 2 cups of water for five minutes. When noodles are done, put into a strainer, rinse with cold water and let drain for a few minutes, shaking the water out to make them as dry as possible.

Cut *tofu* into sugar-cube sized pieces. Cut onion and green pepper into similarly small pieces. Saute in oil together in wok or skillet. (If you use a skillet, you will need more oil because of the flat bottom.)

Mix together the pineapple juice, cornstarch, sugar and vinegar, stir well and pour into wok when other ingredients are sauteed sufficiently. Put in chopped pineapple and cook, stirring often until thickened.

Pour over drained noodles in large bowls. Good as an entree as is, this also goes well with Chinese barbecue pork, sliced thin and dipped into hot mustard sauce and sesame seeds. For an accompanying beverage, try your favorite Chinese tea or fine imported Chinese beer.

⊕ Rambalaya

Yes, it's true. This is a Ramen version of Jambalaya. Don't laugh, it tastes just great!

1 Pkg.	*Ramen noodles*
1 small	*Green pepper*
2	*Pimentos, canned*
or	
1 small	*Sweet red pepper*
1 small	*Onion*
1 cup	*Mushrooms, large pieces*
1 stalk	*Celery*
1 Tbsp.	*Oil*
1/2 tsp.	*Paprika*
1 Tbsp.	*Butter*

Pre-heat oven to 300 degrees Fahrenheit. Knead unopened package of Ramen until broken up medium.

In a small saucepan, boil noodles in 2 cups of water for five minutes. When noodles are done, put into a strainer, rinse with cold water and let drain for a few minutes, shaking the water out to make them as dry as possible.

Saute together mushrooms, onions and peppers. If you feel brave, add your favorite hot chili pepper.

Mix all the ingredients together in a greased baking dish. Bake covered at 300 degrees Fahrenheit for one hour.

Serve with corn bread and salad. Also makes a nice side dish to shrimp or crayfish.

⊕ Bamboo Shoot Fantasy

Fresh bamboo shoots are a real delicacy. Even the canned ones are quite good if you get the whole canned shoots. The canned ready-sliced ones have never tasted as good to me.

1 Pkg.	*Ramen noodles*
1 large	*Bamboo shoot (canned or fresh)*
5 med.	*Mushrooms, fresh*
1/2 med.	*Green pepper*
1 small	*Onion*
1	*Flavor packet*
1 1/2 tsp.	*Cornstarch*
1 1/2 Tbsp.	*Oil*

In a small saucepan, boil noodles in 2 cups of water for five minutes. When noodles are done, put into a strainer, rinse with cold water and let drain for a few minutes, shaking the water out to make them as dry as possible.

All the ingredients should be cut into bite-sized pieces, not minced fine. Cut the whole bamboo shoot into 1/8 inch thick slices at a 45 degree angle. If you are lucky enough to have fresh shoots, after slicing, blanch them for about a minute in boiling water as some varieties of shoots can be slightly bitter. Cut a small onion into quarters, removing the tough ends. Cut mushrooms in half only. Peppers should be cut into 3/8 inch strips.

Mix flavor packet, cornstarch and half a cup of cold water together and set aside.

In a wok or cast iron skillet, stir-fry the vegetables in oil on high heat. (If you use a skillet, you will have to use more oil because of the flat bottom.) Keep everything in motion on the hot metal for about 2 minutes.

Pour in the water mixture, stirring first as the cornstarch has a tendency to settle. Mix into the vegetables stirring until thickened, then pour the mixture over the drained noodles in a large bowl. Use soy sauce to taste. Serve with tea and your choice of pickles.

Noodle Harvest

⏻ **Chinese Fried Noodles**

This is a noodle version of Chinese fried rice, a dish that enjoys popularity throughout Asia and America. This particular version retains its distinctively Chinese flavor and can again become fried rice by substituting cooked rice for the cooked noodles.

1 Pkg.	*Ramen noodles, broken up in package*
1/4 cup	*Chopped onions*
1/4 cup	*Chopped green peppers*
1/4 cup	*Sliced mushrooms*
1	*Egg*

Optional:
1/4 cup   Diced cooked pork
1/4 cup   Diced tofu
2 Tbsp.   Slivered almonds

Break noodles in half while still in package.

In a small saucepan, boil noodles in 2 cups of water for five minutes.

When noodles are done, put into a strainer, rinse with warm water and let drain for a few minutes, shaking the water out to make it as dry as possible.

While this is boiling, slice mushrooms into thin slices and chop onions and peppers into medium-sized pieces.

In a small frying pan, fry an egg in a teaspoon of oil, break the yolk and scramble or fry, then cut into small pieces.

In a larger frying pan or *wok,* heat a Tbsp of oil on high heat until it almost starts to smoke. If you are using meat, saute to taste before turning up heat. Throw in vegetables and almonds, if used. Stir fry, tossing often, for two minutes, then throw in fried egg pieces and bean sprouts and stir fry for another 30 seconds.

Drop drained noodles on top of this mixture and quickly sprinkle with contents of flavor packet, then toss and stir fry all together until well mixed, for a minute or so.

Take off heat immediately, serve in a rice bowl or plate and season to taste with soy sauce. A complete meal as it is, serve with Chinese tea.

⏲ Chow Mein

1 Pkg.	Ramen noodles
1/4 cup	Chopped onions
1/4 cup	Chopped green peppers
1/4 cup	Sliced mushrooms
1 Stalk	Celery
1 cup	Fresh mung bean sprouts
1	Small clove of garlic
1 Tbsp.	Oil
1 Tbsp.	Cornstarch
1	Flavor packet
Optional:	
1/4 cup	Diced cooked meat (your favorite)
1/4 cup	Tiny shrimp
1/4 cup	Almonds, cashews or diced tofu

In a small saucepan, boil noodles in 2 cups of water for five minutes. When noodles are done, put into a strainer, rinse with warm water and let drain for a few minutes.

In a cup, put 3/4 cup cold water, cornstarch and flavor packet. Mix well and set aside.

Cut vegetables for visual effect: Cut celery at a 45 degree angle, nice and thin. Slice mushrooms into thin slices. Chop onion and pepper into medium pieces, about 1″, not minced.

Heat oil in a *wok* until it is about to smoke. (You can use a cast iron frying pan but you will need more oil because of the flat bottom.) Throw in onions, peppers, mushrooms, celery and chopped garlic. Stir fry for two minutes.

If you use meat, saute first before adding the other ingredients. Almonds or cashews or *tofu* can also be sauteed briefly at this time.

Throw in fresh bean sprouts at this point and continue stir frying for another 30 seconds.

Stir the water with the cornstarch mixture (it tends to settle) and pour into the frying pan with the vegetables. Boil only long enough to thicken the sauce and take off heat.

Put the drained noodles in a plate or large soup bowl and cover with the chow mein mixture. Season with soy sauce. A complete meal as it is, serve with Chinese tea and an almond or fortune cookie for dessert.

◔ **Indonesian Fried Noodles**

These fried noodles by themselves are delicious. With the peanut sauce it rates as spectacular.

1 Pkg.	*Ramen noodles*
1/4 cup	*Onion,sliced into crescents*
1/4 cup	*Carrots, slivered*
1 cup	*Cabbage, sliced thin*
1 cup	*Mung bean sprouts, fresh*
1 Tbsp.	*Oil*
1	*Flavor packet*
1/2 tsp.	*Curry powder*
1 tsp.	*Soy sauce*

Break up noodles slightly while still in the package. In a small saucepan, boil noodles in 2 cups of water for 5 minutes. When noodles are done, put into a strainer, rinse with cold water and let drain for a few minutes, shaking the water out to make them as dry as possible.

In a wok or large iron skillet, saute the onions until almost transparent, then turn heat on high and stir-fry in the cabbage and the carrots. After a minute or two, add the fresh bean sprouts and sprinkle on the contents of the flavor packet, curry powder and soy sauce.

Add the drained noodles and continue stir-frying until all the ingredients are mixed together.

⊕ Peanut Sauce

1 tsp.	*Oil*
1 tsp.	*Ginger*
1 clove	*Garlic, finely chopped*
1/4 cup	*Onion, finely chopped*
2 Tbsp.	*Peanut butter, chunky*
1/3 cup	*Milk*
1 tsp.	*Honey*
1 Tbsp.	*Lemon juice*
1/2 tsp.	*Tabasco*
1 Tbsp.	*Soy sauce*
1/2 tsp.	*Cayenne*

In a small saucepan, saute the onions and garlic until transparent. Add the rest of the ingredients and mix thoroughly. Simmer on low heat for 10-15 minutes. Thin with additional milk if it is too thick. In Indonesia, coconut milk would be used. Soy milk also works fine.

Put fried noodles and vegetables into a bowl and pour peanut sauce over them.

⊕ Ram Foo Yung

Here is a tasty Egg Foo Yung you can make when you are out of bean sprouts.

1 Pkg.	*Ramen noodles*
1	*Egg*
1	*Scallion, minced*
1/2 cup	*Mushrooms, chopped*
	or Chicken breast, chopped
	or Pork, cooked, chopped
	or Tempeh, chopped
1 Tbsp.	*Flour*
1 Tbsp.	*Oil*
1	*Flavor packet*
1 tsp.	*Cornstarch*
1/2 cup	*Water*

Knead unopened package of Ramen until broken up fine.

In a small saucepan, boil noodles in 2 cups of water for five minutes. When noodles are done, put into a strainer, rinse with cold water and let drain for a few minutes, shaking the water out to make them as dry as possible.

In a *wok* on medium heat, saute your choice of chopped food - mushrooms, chicken, pork or *tempeh* - adding scallions when almost done.

In a separate bowl, mix together the cooled, drained noodles, stirring in the flour well. When the saute is done, throw them into this mixture. In a wok, fry in enough oil for a 4 inch diameter patty.

Because of the shape of the wok, the patty becomes lens-shaped, and a small amount of oil can properly do the job. In a skillet, you will have to make a flat patty and use a bit more oil. Cook on both sides until firm and golden brown. Drain on newspaper covered with paper towel.

Make a gravy by mixing the flavor packet and cornstarch in water. Bring to a boil, stirring frequently, then cooking until it thickens. Pour immediately onto the patties on a large plate. Serve with hot cooked rice and Chinese tea.

OUR FOUNDER

⊕ Arabic Noodles With Rice

A traditional New Year's dish in many Arabic countries, this carries with it a wish for prosperity and fertility.

1 Pkg.	*Ramen noodles*
1/4 cup	*Rice, uncooked*
1/2 cup	*Onion, minced*
1 Tbsp.	*Butter*
1 cup	*Chick peas, canned*
1 Tbsp.	*Oil*
	Salt, to taste

Knead unopened package of Ramen noodles until broken up fine.

Wash the rice in cold water and drain well.

Fry the onions in the butter until transparent, then add the dry, crushed Ramen noodles and fry lightly until coated with butter. Add the washed, drained rice and also stir and toss well until coated. Add more oil if necessary.

Add one cup of water and simmer for about 20 minutes, or until the rice is fluffy and has absorbed all the water. Add the chick peas while hot.

Serve with a Cucumber-yogurt Salad. (See page 44)

Noodles With Greek Celery Sauce

1 Pkg.	*Ramen noodles*
3 Tbsp.	*Onion, minced*
2 Tbsp.	*Tomato paste*
1/2 cup	*White wine*
4 Tbsp.	*Celery root, minced*
1 Tbsp.	*Butter*
	Salt, pepper to taste
	Romano cheese, grated

In a small saucepan, boil noodles in 2 cups of water for five minutes. When noodles are done, put into a strainer, rinse with cold water and let drain for a few minutes, shaking the water out to make them as dry as possible.

Brown the onions in butter, then add 1/2 cup of water, tomato paste and 1/2 cup of white wine.

Add the minced celery root, salt and pepper, cook until the celery is tender.

Pour over the drained Ramen noodles on a plate or wide bowl and sprinkle with grated *Romano* cheese

⊕ Spanakoramen

Here is a noodle variation of *Spanakopita*, a Greek dish sometimes called "spinach pie". The flavor is similar but the preparation time is much shorter.

1 Pkg.	*Ramen noodles*
1/2 cup	*Feta cheese, crumbled*
1 Pkg.	*Spinach, frozen, 10 oz.*
1/2 cup	*Onion, chopped*
1	*Flavor packet*
1 Tbsp.	*Olive oil*
1 tsp.	*Parsley, dried*
1/2 tsp.	*Basil*

Knead unopened package of Ramen noodles until broken up fine. Boil noodles in 2 cups of water for 5 minutes. When noodles are done, rinse in strainer with cold water and let drain a few minutes, to make them as dry as possible.

Thaw and drain frozen spinach. Chop up fine. Squeeze out excess water.

In a *wok* or iron skillet, saute onions over medium heat until transparent. Turn heat to high and stir-fry spinach for 2 minutes. Add noodles, mix and stir-fry for another minute.

Add parsley, basil and one-half the contents of flavor packet. Take off heat and add crumbled *Feta* cheese. Mix well together. Taste before adding rest of flavor packet so as not to overpower the flavor of the cheese and spinach.

This can be served with fresh sliced tomatoes and a piece of oven-warmed *Pita* bread, or as a great side dish with lamb.

70

The width of the Parthenon is the total length of noodles in one package of instant Ramen.

⏀ Savory Ramen Custard

This is a hearty casserole that is easy to make and delicious.

1 Pkg.	*Ramen noodles*
1	*Egg*
1 Tbsp.	*Fresh parsley, minced*
1/4 tsp.	*Pepper*
1/8 tsp.	*Tabasco or hot sauce*
1/4 cup	*Cream*
1/2 cup	*Low fat small curd cottage cheese*
1 Tbsp.	*Margarine or butter*
3 Tbsp.	*Parmesan or Romano cheese, finely grated*
1/3 cup	*Stock (1/3 cup water mixed with 1/2 flavor packet)*

Preheat oven to 350 degrees Fahrenheit. Grease a small shallow oven dish with oil, butter, or margarine. You can use a 7 inch glass pie plate, or individual ramekin or souffle dish, or small custard mould.

In a small saucepan, boil noodles in 2 cups of water for only 1 1/2 minutes, or until half cooked. Put noodles into a strainer, rinse with cold water and let drain for a few minutes, shaking the water out to make them as dry as possible. Spread Ramen in bottom of baking dish.

In a bowl, combine egg and cottage cheese. Then add pepper, tabasco, cream, stock, parsley and 1-1/2 Tbsp. *Romano* or *Parmesan* cheese. Mix together thoroughly.

Pour mixture over Ramen. Dot with butter or margarine. Sprinkle the rest of the grated cheese on top.

Bake uncovered 40 minutes or until custard is set and top is browned slightly. Cool a few minutes and serve in baking dish or unmold by running a knife around the edge and lifting out with a spatula. Serve with warm dinner rolls and a salad.

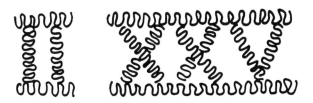

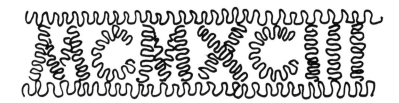

Ramen numerals

Ramen Moussaka

Here is a vegetarian Ramen version of this magnificent Mediterranean dish. Although still by no means low in fat, this treatment solves the problem of excessive oil being absorbed by the eggplant in traditional moussaka recipes. Here the eggplant slices are not fried, but steamed, which also gets rid of any bitterness.

2	Eggplants, large
1 Pkg.	Ramen noodles
1	Flavor packet
1 cup	Water
16 oz. can	Tomatoes, drained and chopped
3 Tbsp.	Tomato Paste
3 Tbsp.	Olive oil
1	Onion, chopped
4 Cloves	Garlic, minced
1/4 cup	Parsley, minced
2 Tbsp.	Butter or margarine
2 Tbsp.	Flour
1	Egg, slightly beaten
1 1/2 cup	Milk
1/4 tsp.	Cinnamon
1/4 tsp.	Garam masala or allspice
1/4 lb.	Gruyere cheese, sliced thin
Dash	Nutmeg
Dash	Black pepper

Preheat oven to 350 degrees Fahrenheit.

Slice the eggplants into 1/2" thick rounds, cover and steam over high heat for 5 to 7 minutes. Uncover and let stand.

Bring 1 cup of water and flavor packet to boil in saucepan. Cook ramen for 5 minutes. Remove from heat and let stand.

In a skillet, fry onions and garlic in 3 Tbsp. olive oil until soft. Remove from heat and add ramen, tomatoes, tomato paste, parsley, cinnamon, garam masala and pepper.

In a saucepan, heat butter and flour until golden. Add milk and continue to heat. Add egg, nutmeg and dash of pepper, stirring constantly as sauce begins to thicken. Remove from heat.

In a deep casserole dish that has been lightly oiled with olive oil, lay down a layer of eggplant slices.

Next, make a layer of half of the ramen-tomato mixture. Cover this with a layer of cheese slices.

Repeat with a layer of eggplant, the rest of the ramen mixture, and another layer of cheese. Finish with a layer of eggplant.

Pour the white sauce over the top layer. Bake uncovered for 1 hour at 350° F. You may need to put a cookie sheet or aluminum foil on another oven rack beneath the casserole to catch any liquid that bubbles over.

By the time you've washed all the dishes you just used and cleaned up the kitchen, the moussaka will be ready. It's quite a project, but the taste is really worth it! Garbanzo Salad (Page 41) and Cucumber-Yoghurt Salad (Page 44) make good side dishes.

Curried Noodles

This dish is an adaptation of Indian cuisine. Once you make this simple meal, you will begin to see the possibilities of endless variations. Try it with other vegetables, *tofu* or meat.

1 Pkg.	*Ramen noodles*
1/4 cup	*Onions, chopped*
1	*Potato, med size, diced*
1	*Carrot, med size, 1/4" slices*
1/4 cup	*Frozen peas*
1	*Flavor packet*
1 tsp.	*Curry powder*
1 Tbsp.	*Cornstarch*

In a small saucepan, boil noodles in 2 cups of water for five minutes. When noodles are done, put into strainer, rinse with warm water and let drain for a few minutes.

In another small saucepan, put the potato, onion, carrot, flavor packet and curry powder and boil gently for 15 minutes. Mix 1 Tbsp. cornstarch in 1/4 cup of water and stir well.

When vegetables are done, add frozen peas and the cornstarch mixture, bring back to a boil until thickened and pour over noodles on a plate or in a large bowl.

A complete meal as it is, serve with hot black tea, like Darjeeling, spiced with three crushed cardamon seeds and laced with cream and sugar. A cold fruit drink, like mango juice, would also enhance this dish.

Hungarian Noolash

1 Pkg.	Ramen noodles
1/2	Flavor packet
1 Tbsp.	Garlic, minced
1 med.	Onion, thin sliced
2 med.	Carrots, thin sliced
1/4 cup	Green pepper, chopped
1/4 cup	Mushrooms, sliced
1 cup	Beef or Seitan*, sliced
2 Tbsp.	Oil
1/2 tsp.	Hot Paprika or Cayenne
pinch	Marjoram
1-1/2 tsp.	Sweet Paprika
1 Tbsp.	White wine
1/2 tsp.	Caraway seeds
1-1/2 tsp.	Tomato paste
1 Tbsp.	Flour
2 Tbsp.	Yogurt or Sour cream

*A Wheat-derived meat substitute

Heat oil in 2 qt. saucepan on medium-high heat. Add meat or *seitan.* If *seitan,* stir frequently until it just starts to stick to pan. Stir in hot paprika and marjoram. Add garlic, onions, green pepper, carrots and mushrooms. Saute, stirring frequently for 5 minutes. Watch bottom of pan. Add water if *seitan* darkens. Add 3/4 cup water, 1/2 flavor packet, wine, tomato paste, sweet paprika and caraway seeds. Cook on low heat for 15 minutes.

78

Break Ramen into quarters while still in package and add to mixture for the last 5 minutes. Mix flour in 1/4 cup cold water and add to mixture, stir until thickened. Whisk in yogurt or sour cream just before serving. A green salad or cold bean salad would complement this nicely.

Ramen Ewe

⏲ Austrian Style Noodles

1 Pkg.   *Ramen noodles*
2 Tbsp.   *Butter*
1/4 cup   *Bread crumbs, dry*
              Salt and pepper to taste

In a small saucepan, boil noodles in 2 cups of water for five minutes. When noodles are done, put into a strainer, rinse with warm water and let drain for a few minutes, shaking the water out to make it as dry as possible.

In a cast iron frying pan, melt 1 Tbsp. of butter. Sprinkle in bread crumbs, mix into butter with a fork and fry, mixing frequently, until almost brown.

Take pan off the burner, scoot the breadcrumbs over to one side and put another Tbsp. of butter on the empty half of the pan.

Put the noodles into the melted butter and stir together before mixing in the bread crumbs. Get the bread crumbs mixed thoroughly into the noodles and saute briefly.

Not exactly diet food, but a rich, nostalgic European variation on Ramen noodles that won't hurt you if you don't make a habit of it. Try a quick lunch of German style wurst (sausage, or try vegetarian soy-based sausage), pickles, bread and butter and a stein of beer with these noodles. The wurst can be boiled along with the noodles to save time.

Don't substitute margarine for the butter. Real butter gives it a fine flavor while margarine makes it quite bland.

Ramen With Fresh Basil Sauce

Here is a great dish from southern France that you can make when basil is in season. It can be made also with frozen basil. Sorry, powdered basil just doesn't make it.

1 Pkg.	*Ramen noodles*
1 tsp.	*Olive oil*
7	*Basil leaves, fresh*
1/2 clove	*Garlic*
2 tsp.	*Butter*
2 Tbsp.	*Cream, heavy*
	Parmesan cheese,
	Salt and pepper to taste

In a small saucepan, cook Ramen noodles in two cups of water, boiling for three minutes. Pour in olive oil. Drain in a colander and return to saucepan.

While waiting for the noodles to cook, chop basil and garlic. Add to drained noodles along with cream and butter. Mix all together and serve in a soup plate. Sprinkle with Parmesan cheese.

Italian Spaghetti

1 Pkg.	*Ramen noodles*
1/2 cup	*Onion, chopped*
1 Clove	*Garlic, minced*
1/2 cup	*Mushrooms, chopped*
1/4 cup	*Green peppers, chopped*
1 Tbsp.	*Olive oil*
16 oz can	*Tomatoes, stewed*
1 Tbsp.	*Tomato paste*
1	*Flavor packet*
	Salt and pepper to taste
	Grated Romano or Parmesan cheese

Boil noodles in 2 cups of water for 5 minutes. When noodles are done, put into a strainer, rinse with warm water and let drain for a few minutes.

Drain tomatoes, reserving the liquid, and chop. Saute onions, garlic, peppers and mushrooms in olive oil in another small saucepan.

When onions are translucent, add tomatoes, tomato paste, 1 cup of tomato liquid and flavor packet. Bring to a boil and simmer for 20 minutes. Add more tomato liquid if necessary.

Pour sauce over noodles on a plate, sprinkle with grated cheese. Good with a piece of garlic bread and, go ahead, have a glass of red wine. *Delicioso!* Almost like back in the old country!

The height of the tower of Pisa is the total length of noodles in 1¾ packages of Ramen

Ramenesque Architecture

⊕ Zucchini-Nut Noodle Sauce

Believe it or not, this unusual combination is a traditional Italian dish. I'll bet you will like it.

1 Pkg.	*Ramen noodles*
2 Tbsp.	*Cream*
2 Tbsp.	*Ricotta cheese*
1 med.	*Zucchini*
1 Tbsp.	*Butter*
1/4 cup	*Walnuts, chopped*
1 dash	*Garlic powder*
1 dash	*Parsley*
1 dash	*Oregano*
	Salt and pepper to taste

In a small saucepan, boil noodles in 2 cups of water for five minutes. When noodles are done, put into a strainer, rinse with cold water and let drain for a few minutes, shaking the water out to make them as dry as possible.

Cut zucchini into sugar-cube size pieces. Put into boiling water and cook for three minutes and drain.

Put the rest of the ingredients in a blender and blend until they are a smooth cream.

Saute the drained zucchini in butter in a cast iron skillet or wok until almost brown. Add the blended ingredients and heat until hot but not boiled.

Pour the topping over the drained Ramen noodles. You may sprinkle the top with some toasted walnuts as a garnish.

85

☉ Ramen Ronaldo

Here is my own version of *Fettucine Alfredo*. I decided to name it after myself. If Alfredo can get away with it, so can I.

1 Pkg.	*Ramen noodles*
1 Tbsp.	*Butter*
1 Tbsp.	*Flour*
1/3 cup	*Milk or Cream*
1/2 tsp.	*Garlic powder*
1 dash	*Nutmeg*
3 Tbsp.	*Romano or Parmesan cheese*
	Salt and pepper to taste

In a small saucepan, boil noodles in 2 cups of water for five minutes. When noodles are done, put into a strainer, rinse with cold water and let drain for a few minutes, shaking the water out to make them as dry as possible.

In another small saucepan, make a white sauce by frying the flour in the butter on medium heat until golden brown. Stir frequently with a fork or whisk.

Pour in milk and spices and cook until thickened. Pour over noodles in a plate and sprinkle with the *Romano* or *Parmesan* cheese, grated.

I like to put about a half-cup of frozen peas in the noodles just before removing from heat. Served with warm garlic bread and red wine, this is an elegant quick snack.

Guacaramen

1 Pkg.	*Ramen noodles*
1 Med.	*Avocado, chopped fine*
1 Med.	*Tomato, diced fine*
1 Small	*Scallion, chopped fine*
2 Tbsp.	*Mayonnaise*
1 Tbsp.	*Lemon or Lime juice*
1/2 tsp.	*Garlic powder*
1/4 tsp	*Flavor packet*
1/4 tsp.	*Coriander, ground*

In a small saucepan, boil noodles in 2 cups of water for five minutes. When noodles are done, put into a strainer, rinse with cold water and let drain for a few minutes, shaking the water out to make them as dry as possible.

Mix all the ingredients except the noodles together thoroughly. Now add noodles and mix thoroughly again.

Goes well with a *burrito* or *taco.* Serve cold.

Ramen Hood and his feudal noodles

Ramen Rarebit

1 Pkg.	Ramen noodles
1/2 cup	Beer, Ale or Stout
1/2 cup	Cheddar cheese, shredded
1 Tbsp.	Butter
1 Tbsp.	Flour
1/4 tsp.	Mustard, dry
1/4 tsp.	Curry powder
1/2 tsp.	Worcestershire sauce
	Salt and pepper to taste

In a small saucepan, boil noodles in 2 cups of water for five minutes. When noodles are done, put into a strainer, rinse with cold water and let drain for a few minutes, shaking the water out to make them as dry as possible.

Mix flour, dry mustard, curry and Worcestershire sauce into cold beer and bring slowly to a boil, stirring often with a wooden spoon. When thickened, add cheese and cook, stirring, until melted. Pour over drained noodles in a bowl.

Serve with a steamed green vegetable like asparagus, broccoli or Brussels sprouts that can be dipped into the sauce. For a tasty beverage, consume the unused portion of the beer, ale or stout, of course.

⊕ Noodle Ramenoff

1 Pkg.	*Ramen noodles*
1/4 cup	*Chopped onions*
1 cup	*Large fresh mushrooms, sliced*
1 Tbsp.	*Butter*
1/3 cup	*Sour cream*
1 Tbsp.	*White wine*
1	*Flavor packet*
1 Dash	*Worcestershire sauce*
1/4 tsp	*Dill weed*
1 Dash	*Paprika*
1 Dash	*Nutmeg*
	Black pepper and salt to taste

Optional:
1/2 cup	*Strips of cooked lean beef or steak*

Boil noodles in 2 cups of water for 5 minutes. When noodles are done, rinse in strainer with warm water and drain for a few minutes.

While noodles are boiling, saute onions until transparent. If you opt for the meat, saute it for a few minutes before doing the onions. Add pepper, nutmeg, paprika and dill weed, then saute mushrooms for 1 minute.

Add 2 tablespoons water, wine and flavor packet, mix well then add sour cream, heat slightly and take off heat. Do not boil sour cream as it will curdle.

Put noodles in a plate or soup bowl and pour the sauce over them. Serve with black bread and tea, and a side dish of steamed

The Ramenoffs

⏲ Spanish Noodles

Wait a minute, there's no such thing as Spanish noodles! Well, there is now! It's just our old friend, Spanish Rice, in a recipe adapted to Ramen noodles. It goes well as a side dish to most Mexican foods like Enchiladas, Tacos, Burritos, etc., or can be served as a main dish, with Refried Beans as a companion.

1 Pkg.	*Ramen noodles*
1 can	*Stewed tomatoes (14-1/2 oz)*
1/4 cup	*Chopped onions*
1/4 cup	*Chopped green pepper*
1/4 tsp.	*Chili powder*
1/4 tsp.	*Basil*
1	*Flavor packet*
1 Tbsp.	*Oil*
1/4 cup	*Monterey Jack cheese, grated*

Saute onions in a medium saucepan until almost transparent. Add chopped green pepper and saute for another minute.

Add one can of stewed tomatoes, flavor packet, chili powder and basil.

Knead unopened package of Ramen noodles until broken up very fine. Add to the mixture, mix in well, breaking up any large pieces of tomato with a spatula.

Bring to slow boil, stirring frequently as this tends to scorch if left untended. If the mixture looks too dry, cook carefully for a minute before adding additional water as the tomatoes tend to give off more liquid when boiled. Keep covered while cooking, but stir often, checking to see if additional water is needed. Cook for 5 to 7 minutes. The mixture should end up thick, not watery.

Serve with refried beans as a side dish, sprinkle grated cheese over noodles and beans.

Battering Ramen

⊕ **Ramburger**

Vegetarians love this one. With a little bit of imagination this can taste just like a hamburger. Serve it on a bun with ketchup, dill pickle and fried onions.

1 Pkg.	*Ramen noodles*
1	*Egg*
1/4 cup	*Onion, chopped*
1/2 cup	*Chopped walnuts*
1 Tbsp.	*Flour*
1 Tbsp.	*Oil*
1	*Flavor packet*
1/2 tsp.	*Poultry seasoning*
1 Tbsp.	*Steak or Worchestershire sauce*
	Black pepper to taste

Knead unopened package of Ramen noodles until broken up real fine. Boil noodles in 2 cups of water for 5 minutes. When noodles are done, drain and rinse with cold water and let drain for a few minutes to make it as dry as possible.

Chop onions and nuts finely and saute in an iron skillet. While frying, add black pepper and poultry seasoning.

In a bowl, mix together egg, flour, A-1 sauce and contents of flavor packet. Add drained noodles, sauteed ingredients and mix well again.

Cook in an oiled skillet on medium heat until browned, then turn over and brown other side. Use a cover on the skillet to get them to cook evenly. The mixture can be shaped neatly into individual patties before they firm up.

⏁ **Ramen Meat Loaf**

1 Pkg.	*Ramen noodles, crushed fine*
1 Lb.	*Lean ground beef*
1/2 cup	*Onion, chopped fine*
2 Cloves	*Garlic, minced*
2	*Eggs, slightly beaten*
1	*Flavor packet*
2 1/2 cups	*Water*
2 Tbsp.	*Parsley, chopped fine*
1 Tbsp.	*Worchestershire sauce*
1/4 cup	*Catsup*
	Oil or butter
	Salt and pepper to taste

Preheat oven to 375 degrees Fahrenheit. Bring 1 1/2 cups water to boil and cook noodles for 3 minutes. Drain.

Dissolve flavor packet in 1 cup water. Grease a loaf-sized baking dish with oil or butter.

In a large bowl mix together all ingredients except catsup. Put in loaf pan, smooth top and spread top with catsup.

Bake at 375 degrees Fahrenheit for 1 hour. Serve warm, or chill in refrigerator for sandwiches.

⦿ Chili Con Ramen

It seems to me that there are as many chili recipes as there are Texans. Well, here's another! Although the cooking takes time, the preparation is fast and simple.

1 Pkg.	*Ramen noodles, crushed*
16 oz can	*Pinto beans and liquid*
16 oz. can	*Whole tomatoes and liquid*
1 cup	*Ground beef or meat substitute*
1/2 cup	*Onion, chopped*
1/2 cup	*Green pepper, chopped*
1 Clove	*Garlic, minced*
2 Tbsp.	*Butter*
1 Tbsp.	*Chili powder*
1	*Flavor packet*
1 Tsp.	*Cumin*
	Salt and cayenne pepper to taste.

Sautee beef, onion, garlic and green pepper together in a medium saucepan over medium high heat until beef is browned through.

Chop up tomatoes and add with their liquid to saucepan. Add beans and their liquid.

Crush noodles in package until granular, and add to saucepan along with other ingredients.

Cook on low heat for 15 minutes, stirring frequently to prevent scorching, if you are in a hurry. If you have the time, let it cook very slowly for up to an hour, stirring from time to time, and the flavors will blend nicely. If you really have will power, put it in the fridge overnight and eat it the next day, when it will really taste the best.

For a vegetarian version, just leave out the meat, or substitute 1/2 cup textured vegetable protein (TVP) or a chopped-up veggie burger. If you use TVP you will need to add some water, as it absorbs a lot of liquid when it reconstitutes.

Serve this chili with corn bread and a big bottle of cold beer. Bon appetit, Podner!

Noodle Dude

◷ Carrot Gravy On Noodles

My favorite gravy. It also goes well on meat, potatoes, steamed vegetables, rice, *cous-cous* and other grains. Once I tried it on plain Ramen noodles, and another great dish was born. Gravy lovers, give this a try!

1 Pkg.	*Ramen noodles*
1/2 cups	*Carrots, sliced thin*
1/2 cups	*Water*
1/2 cup	*Onions, chopped*
1 Clove	*Garlic, minced*
1/2 tsp.	*Curry powder*
1/2 tsp.	*Cornstarch*
1	*Flavor packet*
	Salt and pepper to taste

In a small saucepan, boil noodles in 2 cups of water for five minutes. When noodles are done, put into a strainer, rinse with cold water and let drain for a few minutes.

In a separate saucepan, cook carrots, onions, garlic, curry powder and flavor packet in 1/2 cups of water for about ten minutes, or until carrots are very tender.

Stir cornstarch well into 1/4 cup of cold water and add to mixture, cooking over medium-high heat until thickened.

Pour gravy over noodles, and anything else that happens to be on your plate.

⊕ Ramen Vegetable Loaf

This loaf, great in sandwiches or smothered in gravy, is based on soy grits. You can make your own soy grits by putting dry soy beans through a hand mill or grinder. They cook much faster than whole beans.

1 Pkg.	Ramen noodles
2 cups	Soy grits, cooked
2	Eggs, slightly beaten
1 Tbsp.	Butter or margarine
3 Tbsp.	Flour
1	Flavor packet
1 Tsp.	Poultry seasoning
2 Tbsp.	Soy sauce
1 1/2 cup	Onion, chopped
1 1/2 cup	Green pepper, chopped
2 Stalks	Celery, chopped fine
2 Cloves	Garlic, minced
1/2 cup	Tomato catsup
	Salt and pepper to taste

Preheat oven to 375 degrees Fahrenheit. Bring soy grits to boil in 4 cups of water, lower to medium heat and cook for 20 minutes. Drain. Break up Ramen in package until granular. Boil in 2 cups of water for 5 minutes. Drain.

Fry together onion, garlic, green pepper and celery in butter.

Put all ingredients into a bowl and mix together well. Put into well-greased loaf pan. Bake for 1 1/4 hours at 350° Fahrenheit.

⊕ Ramelet

What's a Ramelet? Why, it's an omelet made with Ramen noodles! This turns out to be a great combination because the eggs are mixed with warm noodles before frying, and most experienced cooks will agree that ice-cold eggs from the refrigerator make a poor omelet. You will be proud of your results from this recipe.

1 Pkg.	*Ramen noodles*
2	*Eggs*
2 Tbsp.	*Milk or cream*
1 tsp.	*Oil*
Additions to Ramelet:	
1/4 cup	*Onions, chopped*
1/4 cup	*Cheese, Cheddar or Swiss, grated*
1/4 cup	*Chopped mushrooms*
1/4 cup	*Chicken, Seafood, or Ham, cooked and diced*

Knead unopened package of Ramen noodles until broken up fine.

In a small saucepan, boil noodles in 2 cups of water for five minutes. When noodles are done, put into a strainer, rinse with warm water and let drain for a few minutes, shaking the water out to make them as dry as possible.

Saute the meat or seafood first, then add onions and mushrooms, saute until the onions are almost transparent, then set aside.

Put the cooked noodles in a small mixing bowl, break the eggs over them and add milk and the contents of the flavor packet. Mix well together.

Heat oil in a skillet to medium heat. Pour in the noodle and egg mixture and pat with a spatula into a uniform thickness. Cover with the lid.

Add the fried mixture and the cheese to the skillet, spreading evenly over the egg mixture.

When the top of the eggs just starts to get cooked, and the cheese is melted, turn half of the omelet over to the other half to give the two halves a chance to cook together.

Serve with sliced tomatoes, buttered toast and a cup of coffee.

Yankee noodle

⊕ Mee Krob

This tasty dish from Thailand normally calls for vermicelli rice noodles, but Ramen works very well, too. It has three components: the noodles, the sauce, and the garnish.

1 Pkg.	*Ramen noodles*
2 Tbsp.	*Lemon or Lime juice*
2 Tbsp.	*Sugar*
1 Tbsp.	*Soy sauce*
1 Tbsp.	*Rice vinegar*
1 Tbsp.	*Sweet rice wine (Mirin)*
1 Tbsp.	*Water*
1/2 tsp.	*Flavor packet*
4 Tbsp.	*Oil*
2 Tbsp.	*Onions, minced*
2 Cloves	*Garlic, minced*
Dash	*Chili powder or Cayenne*
1	*Egg, slightly beaten*
1/2 cup	*Fresh bean sprouts*
1	*Green onion, chopped fine*
	Oil for deep frying

Put the Ramen in warm water and soak for 20 minutes. Drain thoroughly.

Mix the lemon juice, sugar, soy sauce, rice vinegar, *mirin*, water, chili powder and flavor packet in a small bowl.

Next, heat 2 Tbsp. oil in a frying pan, add egg and bean sprouts and scramble together until egg becomes firm. Remove from heat and set aside.

In a small saucepan, heat 2 Tbsp. oil and fry the minced onions and garlic until soft.

Add the sauce and cook over medium heat until the sugar begins to crystallize and the sauce thickens. Remove from heat and set aside.

Heat frying oil to 350 degrees Fahrenheit. Don't overheat, or the noodles will burn.

Deep-fry the drained Ramen noodles in batches, about a handful at a time, for about 1 minute, or until they begin to have a very light golden color. Keep them moving in the oil, turning them frequently. Drain on paper towels.

Put the fried Ramen in a bowl and add the sauce. Toss lightly, using a fork. Try not to break the noodles up too much.

Add the egg/bean sprout mixture and green onion and toss again carefully.

Serve with Thai-style iced coffee, brewed very strong and flavored with cream and sugar, or sweetened condensed milk.

Armenian Wheat-Noodle Pilaf

1 Pkg.	Ramen noodles
1/2 cup	Onion, chopped
1 cup	Bulgur wheat
1	Flavor packet (chicken flavor)
2 Tbsp.	Olive oil

Knead unopened package of Ramen noodles until broken up fine.

In a large saucepan, saute the onion in olive oil until transparent. Add dry noodles and dry *bulgur* wheat and saute until they are all coated with oil. Brown lightly.

Add two cups of water and the contents of the flavor packet and bring to a boil. Stir frequently. Reduce heat to low and simmer. Simmer covered for about 20 minutes or until the wheat is tender and the liquid is all absorbed.

Serve as a side dish to a meat course or have as a lunch with a salad and cheese slices.

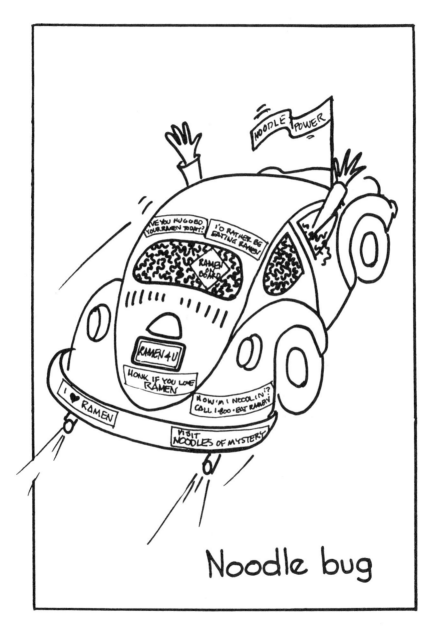

Noodle bug

⏁ **Ramen Quiche**

This is not a fast dish, although it is surprisingly simple and straightforward. It's guaranteed to get rave reviews at the next potluck. Don't be afraid of the pie crust; it's been bachelor-tested.

CRUST

1 cup	*Flour, unbleached white*
1/4 cup	*Oil*
1/3 cup	*Water*
1/4 tsp.	*Salt*

Mix flour and salt together while dry, then add oil and water. Mix together gently, coaxing the ingredients together rather than kneading. This is the secret of light crust: Don't knead! When a dough begins to form as the liquid is absorbed, pick it up in your hands and press it gently into a ball. Then let it sit for 5 minutes.

Now, you can turn this into a difficult project by trying to roll out the dough with a rolling pin, but the easy way is to press it into a 9 inch glass pie plate with the fingers and the heel of the hand until it looks like the pie shell your mother used to make. (Did you wash your hands?) You can even flute the edges if you feel creative.

And the glass pie plate? Yes, it really makes a difference.

FILLING

1 Pkg.	*Ramen noodles*
2	*Eggs*
1-1/3 cups	*Milk or Cream*
1/4 cup	*Swiss cheese, grated*

Pre-heat oven to 450 degrees Fahrenheit.

In a small saucepan, boil noodles in 2 cups of water for five minutes. When noodles are done, put into a strainer, rinse with cold water and let drain for a few minutes, shaking the water out to make them as dry as possible.

Spread noodles evenly on the bottom of the pie shell and sprinkle with the cheese.

Heat milk in a small sauce pan until scalded. Remove from heat and break two eggs into pan with the contents of the flavor packet. Beat well and pour over noodles and cheese in pie shell.

Put into oven and immediately turn heat down to 350 degrees Fahrenheit and bake for 35 minutes or until top begins to brown slightly. Remove from oven and let cool off until the mixture sets.

After you've tried the plain version as shown in this recipe, try adding any of the following:

> *Fried onions and garlic*
> *Fried mushrooms*
> *Fried bacon pieces or "bacon bits"*
> *Steamed vegetables*

Sprinkle over noodles before adding milk, cheese and egg.

⊕ **Noodle Pie**

A most unique use of noodles makes a great main dish. Add your favorite salad and beverage and dinner is ready.

Crust:

2 cups	Flour, unbleached white
1/2 cup	Oil
1/3 cup	Water
1/2 Tsp.	Salt

Follow crust instructions for Ramen Quiche, page 106. Divide dough into two balls, press half into a 9 inch glass pie plate and roll the other half out for the top crust. If you are new at the pie crust business, I recommend rolling it out on a sheet of waxed paper (dust with flour to keep the rolling pin from sticking to the dough) and flipping it on top of the filled shell.

Filling:

1 Pkg.	Ramen noodles
1 cup	Carrots, thinly sliced
1 cup	Peas, fresh or frozen
1	Onion, large, chopped
1 1/2 Tbsp.	Butter or margarine
1	Flavor packet
1/4 cup	Milk
1 Tbsp.	Flour
	Salt and pepper to taste

Optional:

1/4 cup	Cheddar cheese, grated
1/2 cup	Chopped cooked meat

Break Ramen into small pieces in the package. Boil Ramen and carrots in 2 cups water for 5 minutes. Drain. Fry onions in butter until golden. Mix all ingredients together, sprinkling flour gradually. Pour into the bottom shell and cover with upper crust. Poke a few knife-slit holes into the top to let out steam. Bake at 400° Fahrenheit for 20 minutes. Lower heat to 350° F. and bake for an additional 30 minutes.

Ramen Dolmeh

Versions of this dish range from the Mediterranean to Persia and India. If you can't stand or can't find eggplant, you can stuff zucchini, green peppers or tomatoes instead. This recipe will stuff one large plump eggplant.

1 Pkg.	*Ramen noodles, crushed*
1	*Flavor packet*
1	*Large plump eggplant*
1	*Onion, large, chopped*
4 Cloves	*Garlic, minced*
16 oz. can	*Tomatoes*
1/2 cup	*Garbanzo beans, cooked and chopped coarsely*
3 Tbsp.	*Olive oil*
1 Tbsp.	*Tomato paste*
1/2 Tsp.	*Sugar*
2 Tbsp.	*Lemon juice*
1/2 cup	*Water*
1/4 cup	*Pine nuts*
1/4 Tsp.	*Cinnamon*
1/4 Tsp.	*Allspice or Garam Masala*
	Black pepper to taste

Soak crushed Ramen in water for 5 minutes. Drain.

Cut eggplant in half lengthwise. Scoop out flesh, leaving about 3/4 inch thick wall. Chop the removed eggplant into bite-sized chunks. Salt halves and chunks and let drain in colander to remove bitterness. Rinse after 15 minutes and drain.

Drain canned tomatoes, reserving the liquid. Chop up tomatoes.

In a deep skillet, heat 2 Tbsp. olive oil and fry onions and garlic until soft. Remove 1/2 cup of this mixture and set aside. Add 1 Tbsp. oil and eggplant chunks and fry 5 minutes.

In a mixing bowl combine Ramen, garbanzo beans, pine nuts, 1/2 cup of onion-garlic mixture, 1/2 cup chopped tomatoes, tomato paste, 1/2 flavor packet, cinnamon, allspice and pepper. Mix thoroughly.

Stuff noodle mixture in hollowed-out eggplant halves.

To the mixture in the skillet add rest of chopped tomatoes, lemon juice, other 1/2 flavor packet, sugar and water. Stir.

Set stuffed eggplant halves on mixture in skillet. Cover and simmer over medium heat for 30 minutes.

⊕ Maca-Ramen And Cheese

1 Pkg.	*Ramen noodles*
3/4 cup	*Milk*
3/4 cup	*Grated cheddar cheese*
2 tsp.	*Cornstarch*
	Salt and pepper to taste

In a small saucepan, boil noodles in 2 cups of water for five minutes. When noodles are done, put into a strainer, rinse with warm water and let drain for a few minutes.

While noodles are cooking, grate the cheese. Put the milk into a saucepan and mix in the cornstarch while still cold. (Cornstarch is almost impossible to dissolve in hot liquid.)

Put in the grated cheese and heat, constantly stirring so as not to burn on the bottom of the pan, until thickened. Put in the drained noodles and mix together.

Steamed broccoli flowerets are a great complement to this dish. Serve them separately, garnish over the noodles or mix with them.

Desserts

⊕ **Noodle Pudding**

Just like the rice pudding you loved as a kid, this pudding is sure to please. Made with noodles, it seems especially good.

1 Pkg.	*Ramen noodles*
1/2 cup	*Milk*
2 Tbsp.	*Brown sugar*
1 Tsp	*Butter, soft*
1	*Egg*
Dash	*Salt*
Dash	*Nutmeg*
Dash	*Cinnamon*
1/2 tsp.	*Vanilla*
1/2 tsp.	*Lemon juice*

Pre-heat oven to 350 degrees Fahrenheit.

Knead unopened package of Ramen noodles until broken up fine.

In a small saucepan, boil 2 cups of water for 5 minutes. When noodles are done, put into a strainer, rinse with cold water and let drain for a few minutes, shaking out the water to make it as dry as possible.

Mix all the other ingredients with the cooked noodles in a bowl with a fork.

Grease a small ovenware container and pour contents into it. Bake in a 375 degree Fahrenheit oven for 50 minutes.

Polish Apple-Noodle Pudding

1 Pkg.	Ramen noodles
1	Egg
1 Tbsp.	Butter
1 cup	Applesauce
1 Tbsp.	Sugar
1/4 tsp.	Cinnamon
2 Tbsp.	Bread crumbs

Pre-heat oven to 350 degrees Fahrenheit.

Break noodles in unopened package of Ramen noodles into quarters.

In a small saucepan, boil noodles in 2 cups of water for five minutes. When noodles are done, put into a strainer, rinse with cold water and let drain for a few minutes, shaking the water out to make them as dry as possible.

Mix together noodles, melted butter, egg, sugar, cinnamon and half of the bread crumbs. Butter up the inside of a small glass loaf baking dish and in it place alternate layers of noodle mixture and applesauce, starting and ending with a layer of noodles.

Sprinkle top with breadcrumbs, bake in an oven at 350° Fahrenheit for 25 minutes. Spoon Lemon Sauce (recipe on the next page) over each individual serving.

⏱ **Lemon Sauce**

1/4 cup	*Water*
3 Tbsp.	*Lemon juice*
1 Tbsp.	*Butter*
1 cup	*Powdered sugar, sifted*
1	*Egg*

Bring water, lemon juice and butter to boil in small saucepan.

Whisk in powdered sugar until it is completely dissolved.

Beat in egg, and whisk constantly over medium heat until sauce thickens. Serve as a topping on Polish Apple-Noodle Pudding, previous page, on fruit cake, or even on vanilla ice cream.

Noodle Tootle

⊕ Maple Ramen

This recipe uses maple syrup for a delicious breakfast or dessert ramen dish.

1 Pkg.	*Ramen noodles*
2 Tbsp.	*Butter or margarine*
1/4 cup	*Chopped pecans*
	Maple syrup to taste

In a small saucepan, boil noodles in 2 cups of water for five minutes. When noodles are done, put into a strainer, rinse with warm water and let drain for a few minutes, shaking the water out to make it as dry as possible.

Melt the butter in a cast iron frying pan. Mix drained noodles and pecans together. Pat noodles into several thin, cookie-like shapes. Fry the noodle patties in the pan over medium high heat, turning frequently with a spatula.

When noodles are lightly browned and slightly crispy, turn out onto a plate. Pour on maple syrup to taste. Pretty good, eh?

Orange-Pineapple Cream Ramen

A unique dessert that is quick and easy to make and tastes simply wonderful.

1 1/2 cup	*Orange juice*
1 Pkg.	*Ramen noodles, crushed*
1/4 cup	*Whipped topping*
1/4 cup	*Sour cream*
5 oz. can	*Pineapple chunks, drained*
11 oz. can	*Mandarin oranges, drained*

Bring orange juice to boil. Crush noodles in package and add to orange juice, cover and cook over medium low heat for 10 minutes. Remove from heat, set aside for 5 minutes and let noodles absorb all the liquid.

In a small bowl, mix together whipped topping and sour cream.

Put noodles in a larger bowl. Add topping mixture, pineapple and mandarin oranges and toss well. Can be eaten immediately or chilled.

⊕ Noodles With Prunes

A traditional Jewish dish that adapts very well to Ramen noodles. Sorry, but as far as I know, instant Ramen has not been made to Kosher specifications, so this will have to be termed "Kosher- style".

1 Pkg.	*Ramen noodles*
1 cup	*Prunes, stewed and pitted*
1/2 cup	*Prune juice*
1-1/2 Tbsp.	*Butter*
1-1/2 tsp.	*Sugar*
1/4 tsp.	*Cinnamon*
1/4 cup	*Bread crumbs, dried*

Pre-heat oven to 350 degrees Fahrenheit.

Break noodles in unopened package to medium size pieces.

In a small saucepan, boil noodles in 2 cups of water for five minutes. When noodles are done, put into a strainer, rinse with cold water and let drain for a few minutes, shaking the water out to make them as dry as possible.

Sprinkle prunes with a mixture of sugar and cinnamon. Butter up the inside of a small casserole dish and in it place alternate layers of prunes and noodles starting and ending with a layer of noodles. Pour prune juice over and sprinkle with bread crumbs. Dot the top with butter and bake at 375 degrees Fahrenheit until the crumbs are all browned.

120

⊕ Ramen On A Stick

You're going to feel very silly when you start winding noodles on a stick, but it's really a delicious and novel snack.

1 Pkg.	*Ramen noodles*
8	*Popsicle sticks*
1/4 cup	*Chopped Pecans, Walnuts or Peanuts*
6 oz.	*Caramel candy cubes*
	Oil for deep frying

Use a package that hasn't been broken up so that you get nice long noodles. Boil the noodles in a saucepan with 2 cups of water. Drain in a colander. Carefully wrap one end of a stick with noodles until about 1 1/2 inches in diameter. This is a sloppy mess when the noodles are hot and wet, but gets easier as they cool and dry -- then they begin to stick together. Just try it to get the knack.

Put the caramels (remove the wrappers) in the top part of a double boiler with plenty of water in the bottom part, and boil at medium high. It takes about 1/2 hour until they get gooey; don't let all the water boil away. Add 1 Tbsp. of boiling water to the caramel mixture to speed up the process.

Heat oil to 350° F. Hold the end of a stick in a pair of tongs and deep-fry for a little over 1 minute. Drain on paper towel. Repeat with all the sticks.

When most of the oil has drained off, roll the fried noodles in the softened caramel. Then roll the caramel-covered noodles in the chopped nuts. Let cool on waxed paper. Makes 7 or 8 sticks.

⏲ **Nutty Noodles**

Here is a traditional noodle dessert from Hungary.

1 Pkg.	*Ramen noodles*
1/4 cup	*Walnuts, chopped finely*
1 Tbsp.	*Powdered sugar*
1 Tbsp.	*Butter*
1/2 tsp.	*Lemon juice*

Break noodles in unopened package of Ramen noodles into quarters.

In a small saucepan, boil noodles in 2 cups of water for five minutes. When noodles are done, put into a strainer, rinse with cold water and let drain for a few minutes, shaking the water out to make them as dry as possible. In a bowl, mix drained noodles, melted butter, lemon juice together well. Mix walnuts and confectioner's sugar together and serve as a topping to individual portions of noodles.

Appendix

SOURCES

Here is a list of the products I have used to create my own substitutes for flavor packets:

Maggi Seasoning
Nestle Foods Corporation
Purchase, NY 10577

Vogue Instant Mixes
Vogue Cuisine
Hallandale, FL 33009

Quick-Sip Bouillon Concentrate
(Broth or seasoning powder)
Bernard Jensen Products
Solana Beach CA 92075

Dr. Bronner's Balanced Mineral Bouillon
Rabbi Emanuel H. Bronner
Box 28 Escondido CA 92025

Vegetable Bouillon Cubes, Unsalted
Morga AG
9652 Ebnat-Kappel/Switzerland

Vecon Natural Vegetable Stock
Metabasic Products LTD
Chessington, Surrey, England

Herb-Ox Bouillon Cubes
Pure Food Company, Inc.
Mamaroneck NY 10543

125

NOODLE-OGRAPHY

Here is a list of Ramen manufacturers and distributors. This list can probably never be complete because of the rapid growth of the industry.

Top Ramen
Nissin Foods
Gardena, CA 90249

Demae Ramen
Nissin Foods Gardena, CA 90249

Western Family Ramen
Western Family Foods, Inc.
Portland, OR 97223

Sapporo Ichiban
Sanyo Foods of America
11955 Monarch St.
Garden Grove CA 92641

Westbrae Natural Ramen
Westbrae Natural foods
Berkely, CA 94706

Maruchan Ramen
Maruchan, Inc.
Irvine, CA 92714

Royal Pagoda Ramen
Div. of Preisco Foods, ltd.
Coquitlan, B.C., Canada

Korea-America Foods
San Francisco, CA 94080

Pacific Crest Ramen
Acme Food Sales
Seattle, WA 98108

Tokyo Ramen
Nishimoto Trading Co. Ltd.
Los Angeles, CA 90058

Mitoku Co., Ltd.
Tokyo, Japan 100

Zen Ramen
Anzen Pacific Corp.
Portland, OR 97211

Town House Ramen
Safeway Stores, Inc.
Oakland, CA 94660

Eden
Eden Foods, Inc.
Clinton, MI 49236

Smack Ramen
Sanwa Foods, Inc.
City of Industry, CA 91746

Ramen Noodles (Generic)
Sunfresh Inc.
St. Paul, MN 55107

Ramen Pride
Union Foods
Costa Mesa, CA 92626

Soba Shop Ramen
Westbrae Natural (distributor)
Downey, CA 90240

Index

A

Applesauce, Polish
Apple- Noodle
Pudding, 116
Arabic, Noodles With
Rice, 68
Armenian,
Wheat-Noodle Pilaf,
104
Asparagus,
Asparagus Salad, 43
Austrian, Austrian
Style Noodles,80

B

Bamboo shoots,
Bamboo Shoot
Fantasy, 58
Chop Chae, 54
Beans,
Garbanzo
Arabic Noodles With
Rice, 68
Garbanzo Salad, 41
Green
Chop Chae, 54
Harvest Vegetable
Soup, 32
Pinto, Chili Con
Ramen, 96
Soy, Ramen
Vegetable Loaf, 99
Sprouts
Chinese Fried
Noodles, 60

Chow Mein, 62
Hot-Cold Szechuan
Noodles, 50
Indonesian Fried
Noodles, 64
Mee Krob, 102
Beef
Chili Con Ramen, 96
Chop Chae, 54
Hungarian Noolash, 78
Noodle Ramenoff, 78
Ramen Meat Loaf, 95
Beets, Ramen Borshch,
25
British, Ramen
Rarebit, 89
Broths,
Basic Broth #1, 12
Basic Broth #2, 12
Japanese Fish Stock,
13
Korean Black Bean
Broth, 13
Miso Broth, 13

C

Cabbage,
Indonesian Fried
Noodles, 64
Shredded Cabbage
Salad, 44
Yaki Ramen, 52
Cajun, Rambalaya, 57
Carrots,

Carrot Gravy on
Noodles, 98
Carrot Thread Soup,
27
Chop Chae, 54
Curried Noodles,77
Harvest Vegetable
Soup, 32
Herbed Cream of
Carrot Soup, 28
Hungarian Noolash, 78
Indonesian Fried
Noodles, 64
Shredded Carrot Salad,
44
Ten Minute Stew, 49
Cauliflower,
Cauliflower-Cheese
Soup, 31
Ten Minute Stew, 49
Celery,
Noodles With Greek
Celery Sauce, 69
Cheese,
Cheddar,
Almost
Instantaneous Corn
Chowder, 26
Cauliflower-Cheese
Soup, 31
Maca-Ramen And
Cheese, 112
Ramelet, 100

Feta, Spanakoramen, 70

Monterey Jack, Spanish Noodles, 92

Ricotta, Zucchini-Nut Noodle Sauce, 85

Swiss, Ramen Quiche, 106

Chicken,
Hot-Cold Szechuan Noodles, 50

Ram Foo Yung, 66

Ramelet, 100

Chili powder, Chili Con Ramen, 96

Spanish Noodles, 92

Chinese,
Bamboo Shoot Fantasy, 58

Chinese Cold Noodle Salad, 35

Chinese Fried Noodles, 60

Chow Mein, 62

Hot-Cold Szechuan Noodles, 50

Ram Foo Yung, 66

Sweet-Sour Tofu, 56

Corn, Almost Instantaneous Corn Chowder, 26

Cucumber,
Chinese Cold Noodle Salad, 35

Cucumber-Yoghurt Salad, 44

Noodle Gazpacho, 29

Curry,
Almost Instantaneous Corn Chowder, 26

Carrot Gravy on Noodles, 98

Carrot Thread Soup, 27

Curried Noodles, 77

Indonesian Fried Noodles, 64

Peanut Sauce, 65

E

Eggs,
Chinese Fried Noodles, 60

Chop Chae, 54

Egg Drop Soup, 20

Mee Krob, 102

Noodle Pudding, 115

Polish Apple-Noodle Pudding, 116

Ram Foo Yung, 66

Ramburger, 94

Ramelet, 100

Ramen Vegetable Loaf, 99

Ramen Quiche, 106

Ramen Meat Loaf, 95

Savory Ramen Custard, 72

F

Fish, Also see Seafood Japanese Fish Stock, 13

Flavor packets, 7-15

French, Ramen With Fresh Basil Sauce, 81

Fruits,
Lemon Sauce, 117

Noodles With Prunes, 120

Orange-Pineapple Cream Ramen, 119

Polish Apple-Noodle Pudding, 116

G

Garlic, Charlie's Cold Cure, 24

Ginger, Ginger Ramen Salad, 39

Gravy, Carrot Gravy on Noodles, 98

Greek,
Noodles With Greek Celery Sauce, 69

Spanakoramen, 70

H

Ham,
Chinese Cold Noodle Salad, 35

Ramelet, 100

Hungarian,
Hungarian Noolash, 78

Nutty Noodles, 122

I

Indian, Curried Noodles, 77

Indonesian,
Fried Noodles and Peanut Sauce, 64-65

Italian,
Garbanzo Salad, 41
Italian Spaghetti, 82
Ramen Ronaldo, 86
Tuna-Ramen Salad, 36
Zucchini-Nut Noodle
Sauce, 85

J

Japanese,
Kitsune Ramen, 19
Yaki Ramen, 52
Jewish, Noodles With
Prunes, 120

K

Korean, Chop Chae, 54

L

Lemon,
Lemon Sauce, 117
Nutty Noodles, 122

M

Mandarin orange,
Orange-Pineapple
Cream Ramen, 119
Maple syrup, Maple
Ramen, 118
Meat, See individual
meats
Mediterranean,
Garbanzo Salad, 41
Noodles With Greek
Celery Sauce, 69
Spanakoramen, 70
Mexican,
Chili Con Ramen, 96
Guacaramen, 87
Spanish Noodles, 92

Middle Eastern,
Arabic Noodles With
Rice, 68
Cucumber-Yogurt
Salad, 44
Garbanzo Salad, 41
Mushrooms,
Bamboo Shoot
Fantasy, 58
Chinese Fried
Noodles, 60
Chop Chae, 54
Chow Mein, 62
Hungarian Noolash, 78
Italian Spaghetti, 82
Noodle Ramenoff, 90
Ram Foo Yung, 66
Rambalaya, 57
Ramelet, 100
Ramen Borshch, 25
Saute Stew, 47
Yaki Ramen, 52

N

Nettles,
Nettle Noodles, 22
Pickled Nettle
Greens, 40
Nuts,
Peanuts, Hot-Cold
Szechuan Noodles,
50
Pecans, Maple
Ramen, 118
Ramen on a Stick, 121
Pine Nuts, Ramen
Dolmeh, 110

Walnuts,
Nutty Noodles, 122
Ramburger, 94
Zucchini-Nut Noodle
Sauce, 85

O

Omelet, Ramelet, 100
Oranges,
Orange-Pineapple
Cream Ramen , 119

P

Peanut Butter, Peanut
Sauce, 65
Peas,
Black-eyed, Ashte
Reshte, 23
Green
Curried Noodles, 77
Three Minute Stew,
48
Pepper, Green,
Bamboo Shoot
Fantasy, 58
Chili Con Ramen, 96
Chinese Fried
Noodles, 60
Chow Mein, 62
Hungarian Noolash,
78
Italian Spaghetti, 82
Noodle Gazpacho,29
Rambalaya, 57
Ramen Vegetable
Loaf, 99
Saute Stew, 47

129

Spanish Noodles, 92
Sweet-Sour Tofu, 56
Red, Rambalaya, 57
Persian,
Ashte Reshte, 23
Ramen Dolmeh, 110
Pie,
Crust,
Ramen Quiche, 106
Noodle Pie, 108
Vegetable, Noodle
Pie, 108
Pineapple,
Orange-Pineapple
Ramen, 119
Sweet-Sour Tofu, 56
Polish,
Polish Apple-Noodle
Pudding, 115
Ramen Borshch, 25
Pork,
Chinese Fried
Noodles, 60
Ram Foo Yung, 66
Yaki Ramen, 52
Potato,
Curried Noodles, 77
Harvest Vegetable
Soup, 32
Pudding,
Noodle Pudding, 115
Polish Apple-Noodle
Pudding, 116

R
Russian, Noodle
Ramenoff, 90

S
Seafood, See also Fish
Shrimp,
Chow Mein, 62
Ramen Quiche, 106
Ramelet, 100
Saute Stew, 47
Tuna, Tuna-Ramen
Salad, 36
Sour cream,
Noodle Ramenoff, 90
Orange-Pineapple
Ramen, 119
Ramen Borshch, 25
Soybeans, Ramen
Vegetable Loaf, 99
Spanish,
Noodle Gazpacho, 29
Spanish Noodles, 92
Spinach,
Kitsune Ramen, 19
Spanakoramen, 70
Spinach Noodle Cream
Soup, 30
Spinach-Ramen Salad,
38
Sesame-Spinach Salad,
43
Stocks, See Broths

T
Thai, Mee Krob, 102
Tofu,
Chinese Fried
Noodles, 60
Kitsune Ramen, 19
Sweet-Sour Tofu, 56

Three Minute Stew, 48
Tomato,
Chili Con Ramen, 96
Garbanzo Salad, 41
Guacaramen, 87
Harvest Vegetable
Soup, 32
Italian Spaghetti, 82
Noodle Gazpacho, 29
Spanish Noodles, 92
Spinach-Ramen Salad,
38
Tomato Stew, 51

V
Vegetables, See
individual vegetables
Harvest Vegetable
Soup, 32

Z
Zucchini
Harvest Vegetable
Soup, 32
Ten Minute Stew, 49
Zucchini-Nut Noodle
Sauce, 85

Noodle-oo !

Order Form

For additional copies of The Book of Ramen, visit your local bookstore, or order directly from Turtleback Books:

Name...

Address..

City.. State .... Zip ....

Yes! Please send me _____ copies of The Book of Ramen at $9.95 each. (Washington State residents add $0.80 sales tax per book.) Allow 4 to 6 weeks for delivery.

Subtotal: _____

Shipping: _____

Total:_____

Shipping Information:

☐ Book Post: $2.00 for first book, $1.00 each additional book.

☐ UPS: $3.00 for first book, $1.50 each additional book.

☐ Outside US: $4.00 for first book, $2.00 each additional book.

Send order along with check or money order in US funds to:

Turtleback Books
Post Office Box 2012
Friday Harbor, Washington
U.S.A. 98250